Grand Canyon Nankoweap

Hiking the Notorious Horsethief Trail

Flood Hefley

Johnson Books
Denver

Published by Johnson Books, an imprint of Bower House

Cover design by the author
Text design by D. Kari Luraas
All photos by Flood Hefley unless otherwise noted.

About the cover: The Nankoweap Ruin is located in the east and slightly north facing cliffs of the Nankoweap Mesa. The view is to the south and slightly east downstream of the Colorado River. The "historic" muddy color of the river is due to upstream side canyon flooding and the deposit of rock and sediment into the main stream. Nankoweap Ruin photo courtesy of the Grand Canyon National Park Museum Collection (GRCA D3516). Northern Arizona sky and moon photo by Flood Hefley.

9   8   7   6   5   4   3   2

ISBN: 978-1-55566-456-5
Library of Congress Control Number: 2013943762

Please Note: Risk is always a factor in backcountry and high-mountain travel. Many of the activities described in this book can be dangerous, especially when weather is adverse or unpredictable, and when unforeseen events or conditions create a hazardous situation. The author has done his best to provide the reader with accurate information about backcountry travel, as well as to point out some of its potential hazards. It is the responsibility of the users of this guide to learn the necessary skills for safe backcountry travel, and to exercise caution in potentially hazardous areas. The author and publisher disclaim any liability for injury or other damage caused by backcountry traveling or performing any other activity described in this book.

Printed in Canada

For my wife Kathleen and my kids

Dedicated to Fred "Andy" Anderson
who built my hiking foundation
on the Bright Angel Trail

Fred "Andy" Anderson at
Mather Campground, Grand
Canyon South Rim.

Many thanks to
Steve Bridgehouse,
Grand Canyon National Park
and
Dustin Burger,
Kaibab National Forest,
North Kaibab Ranger District

In memory of
my mom, Selma,
who encouraged me
to keep a
Grand Canyon journal

Thank you to all those who are behind the scenes at Johnson Books, such as Linda Doyle, that made *Grand Canyon Nankoweap* possible. Thank you to my publisher, Mira Perrizo. Under her keen eye, *Grand Canyon Nankoweap* was guided into congruous literary form. A special thank you goes to designer Kari Luraas who profoundly grasped my concept for the book's cover and diligently produced an astounding testimony not only to the Grand Canyon but specifically to the Nankoweap Trail and its iconic archaeological feature.

Also by Flood Hefley

Grand Canyon Trivia Trek:
An Intrepid Rim-to-Rim Historical Journey

CONTENTS

Nankoweap region. While seemingly close to the limited services of Grand Canyon's North Rim, in actuality, the Nankoweap Trail is in a remote region and designated by the National Park Service as a Primitive Use Area. This means the area is recommended for highly experienced Grand Canyon hikers only. Trails and routes are non-maintained and require proven Grand Canyon route-finding ability and there is the potential for little to no contact with other people. En route creeks, springs, and seeps are scarce or absent requiring the ability to pack, carry, and ration drinking water over extraordinary terrain to the next renewable water source.

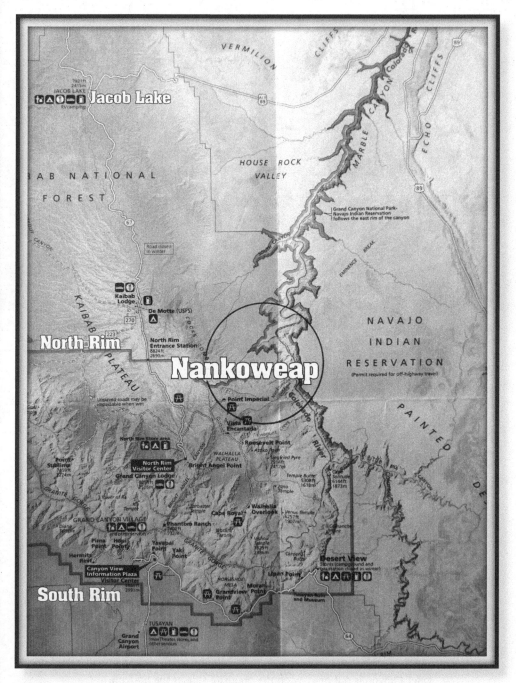

(Map courtesy National Park Service, Grand Canyon National Park. "Circle" and bold white notations added by the author.)

Saddle up. On Forest Development Road 8910, the ever-present saddle of the Saddle Mountain Wilderness is framed within the signposts. From House Rock Valley, the view is southerly where the Inner Canyon is out of view on the opposite side of the horizon.

PREFACE

Grand Canyon Nankoweap: Hiking the Notorious Horsethief Trail provides an explanation of the Nankoweap Trail, its access roads, and its in-way approach routes—Trail #31 and Trail #57—leading to the Grand Canyon National Park's trailhead at Boundary Ridge. My hope is that the text and photographs will be an appropriate extension of the Kaibab National Forest's goals in providing instruction to the route, and the National Park Service's goals for a safe hike once on the Inner Canyon Nankoweap Trail, from start to finish, for those who are "up to the challenge."

The Nankoweap Trail, also known as the Horsethief Trail, is NOT the place to start a first Grand Canyon hike, especially in this remote region where one is removed from chances of other human contact. The National Park Service states that the Nankoweap Trail is the steepest and most difficult of the named routes in the canyon. *It is. Know your limits.* Novice Grand Canyon hikers should perform self-accountable, prerequisite backpack treks on the National Park Service maintained trails. After that, consult the National Park Service and develop a strategic hiking plan to complete the shade-less and waterless South Kaibab Trail round trip.

A part of the South Kaibab Trail round-trip plan would be to cache water on the way in for use on the way out, as would be done on a backcountry route. This should be an accurate gauge as to how a hiker might perform in Grand Canyon's backcountry. The saving aspect of this exercise is the frequency of trail use by other hikers and mule trains, which makes help close at hand. Then advance in a logical manner to the less-traveled routes in Grand Canyon. I'm a weathered Grand Canyon backpacker with decades of both group hiking and solo hiking experience. I devised my solo hiking plan and started my solo hikes as described above.

Depending on *canyoneering* skill levels, it is not uncommon for hikes on the 130-year-old Nankoweap Trail to be aborted due to a fear of heights, encroaching weather, and encounters with trail deterioration. Overestimate the canyon and underestimate your ability. This will make the difference between a wondrous

Geared up. From Ooh Aah Point above O'Neill Butte, South Kaibab Trail round-trip hike. Maintained by the National Park Service, the steep South Kaibab Trail best represents exposure conditions (lack of shade and no renewable water sources) that will be found on the non-maintained backcountry routes. Notice the water cache (backpack left side) in position for immediate en route placement.

journey and an ordeal. **If you have any doubt as to your ability to safely complete a trip, do not attempt it.**

The Nankoweap Trail has more stamina than most backpackers. Hiking in the Grand Canyon is the opposite of hiking in the mountains. In the canyon, there is little or no renewable water sources until a destination is reached, such as the uncommon perennial stream or the Colorado River. In mountain hiking, one starts out fresh and heading uphill with the pressure created by the weight of a full pack and the pull of gravity on the broader heel of the foot. In canyon hiking, one travels downhill first with the pull of gravity first forced on the toes. At the uphill terminus of a mountain hike, there is an about-face and the mountain is descended with a lighter pack and where a stream may be within close access.

Hiking out of a canyon, the pack can weigh more than it did on the hike in, as there will be the need for a greater quantity of drinking water that will outweigh the food brought for the duration of the trek. Also, the trek out of the canyon will be done while hiking up into the "thinner air" of elevation—less oxygen to breathe.

After hiking the Grand Canyon trails and routes for four decades, my challenge on the Nankoweap Trail mostly came from within. (Even with carefully chosen and "broken in" footwear, with upgraded insoles and dynamic socks, I still remember the blisters that I received when I was a youngster starting out in the canyon in the early 1970s.) At Nankoweap Creek I self-treated the blisters on both of my feet with no blame on the equipment or the trail. The blame resides in myself and my desire to hike the extended canyon.

Consult the Grand Canyon National Park Backcountry Information Center and the U.S. Forest Service, North Kaibab Ranger District, for up-to-date weather, entry road and route conditions prior to entering this remote, waterless, exposed, and rugged region within the Kaibab National Forest and the Grand Canyon National Park.

The South Kaibab Trail. The steepness and the lack of shade is especially represented in the trail's midsection switchbacks called the Red and Whites.

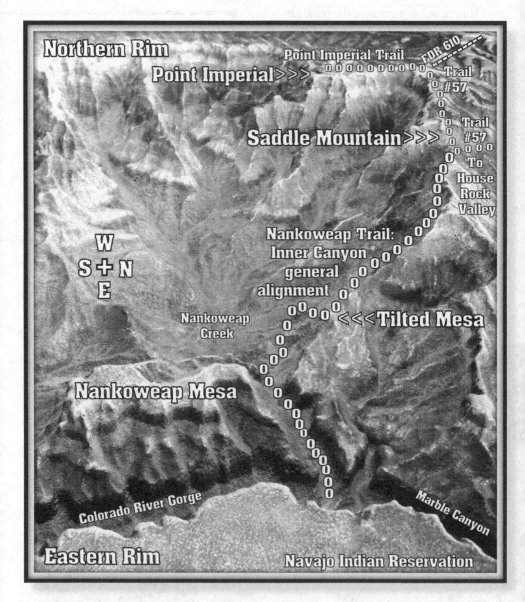

Raised-relief map. Nankoweap Trail general alignment in a westerly view from the east at the Navajo Indian Reservation toward the North Rim at Point Imperial. Raised-relief map terrain representations are exaggerated to assist the visual impact of the terrain features. Three-dimensional representation of Grand Canyon National Park on display at the Yavapai Geology Museum, South Rim. (Map section photo and notations by the author.)

INTRODUCTION

Frederick Dellenbaugh, with John Wesley Powell's second Colorado River expedition, traced the word *Nankoweap* within the Southern Paiute to mean "canyon
of echoes." And that it is. In the middle of a breezy night from high above on the
upper rock assemblage of Tilted Mesa, Nankoweap Creek is aqua-audible as it
laps and utters and whispers on its way to the Colorado River. Where a five-point
buck may be spotted meandering, so does the creek meander at just a few feet
wide and deep in its basalt bed.

My sister Heidi begins the Nankoweap account with her alluring question,
"Did I ever tell you how Flood almost died in the Grand Canyon?" Decades back,
we were on our own backpacking trip to Havasupai (Supai). After checking in
with the tribe, we hiked to the crest of the 100-foot high Havasu Falls and then
to the falls' basin. From our campsite the next day, we walked downstream to the
top of the 200-foot high Mooney Falls. From the waterfall's spillway, I pointed
out the cliff-clinging cavern route to the falls' basin. While I followed closely behind, Heidi began the vertical descent. Emerging out of a shady cavern and passing into the next along the cliff face, gradually but certainly, using the spike and
chain-mounted handholds, we made it to the final section. With our feet now
planted onto Mooney's beach, Heidi exclaimed, "I'm afraid of heights!" I never
knew she was afraid of high places. She went onto say that she was going to "kill
me" for making her go down there. That's how I almost died in the Grand Canyon. The Nankoweap Trail is a non-maintained backcountry route and is not for
anyone with a fear of heights. If you've come to break yourself of acrophobia by
hiking the elevated and exposed drifting ledge-ways, then, unquestionably, you
are in the right place.

In my earlier years in the canyon, I could have rapidly hiked the Nankoweap
Trail, getting it tallied. Yet, I paused to reflect on what the Grand Canyon might
mean to me personally at the age determined by the assistant to the governor
of New Mexico. While I was on my first solo hike of the Tanner Trail in 1982, I
learned from the small group of hikers that accompanied the governor's assistant that he was celebrating his fiftieth birthday. This small group and I met on
the opposite side of the canyon on the Tanner Trail—which just so happens to

be the southern section of the Horsethief Trail. Not quite my twentieth birthday, I decided that hiking the canyon—and being able to—at fifty years of age would be an inspirational goal, while at the time seeming tranquilly distant at more than thirty years away and on the outskirts of my peripheral vision.

In June 2012, I obtained my Backcountry Use Permit. With the first step accomplished, I reassessed and upgraded a few pieces of hiking gear. I had just turned fifty and would be hiking solo. I'd be my own worst enemy and my own buddy system and wingman. Somewhere in between receiving my hiking permit and the beginning of my hike, I rediscovered that Grand Canyon is still my personal physical fitness governor, which prompted me to be on the ready to hike. Of all the named trails and routes I have been on, Nankoweap would be the most challenging. And I would be alone. At this point, it is interesting to note that the varying definition of *Nankoweap* is "humans killed." It is my prerogative to choose the first meaning!

> "Folks call me Old Timer, when I first heerd it, I looks around quick to see if some old guy's behind me. When I seen they's referrin' to me, my hackles riz up. I'm used to the label now. Fact is, I sorta like it. Makes me feel I'm a sure-'nough canyon man."—Hezekiah Appleyard, *Brighty of the Grand Canyon* by Marguerite Henry

In my pickup truck on Arizona State Route 67 and on the apron of the North Rim's forest and meadows, I turn left onto Forest Development Road 611. Against a conifer backdrop, heart-shaped aspen leaves are turning from green to yellow to orange to red. In the gusty winds of autumn's arrival, the wingtip leaves flutter past like clouds of butterflies in an Indian summer. I realize, after contemplating the route for decades, it is time. I also realize that the age of fifty did not hesitate in its arrival, and a personal solo-best awaits me on the Nankoweap Trail.

PERSONAL SAFETY

You are responsible for your own and your group's safety from start to finish.
The following is representative of some, but not all, of the conditions and risks when traveling anywhere in the Grand Canyon and vicinity. Other statements of caution follow throughout the text.

◈ Medical: Many die in the Grand Canyon every year. Help is far away. Possess an understanding of basic field medical treatment. This book provides only an awareness of some of the potential risks of hiking in the Grand Canyon.

◈ The National Park Service states: *"Canyoneering* involves unavoidable risks that every person assumes. Your safety depends on your good judgment based on experience and a realistic assessment of your hiking ability. **If you have any doubt as to your ability to safely complete a trip, do not attempt it."**

◈ Weather conditions also take part in the assessment of your ability to cope with the Grand Canyon's ever-fluctuating climate. It could be cold and raining or snowing on the rims and hot and dry at the bottom of the canyon. Assess appropriate gear needed for safe travel from the rim, no matter how far into the canyon, and back to the rim.

◈ Tell someone where and when you are going as your "check-in service." Stay on your itinerary. Your Backcountry Use Permit is only for the National Park Service's office use. For those who are reported as "overdue" or "missing," the permit is utilized as a search guideline.

◈ Grand Canyon routes change with the coming and going of storms or with the simple aspect of a trail washout, a fallen tree, or the complications of a cliff face collapsing onto a route. Therefore, mileages usually increase rather than decrease in order to negotiate a "terrain break."

◈ Rattlesnakes and scorpions inhabit the canyon. Before stepping in front of a shady alcove or boulder, or using a "hand hold" that may represent a possible reptile den, use a trekking pole to gently probe and investigate for a snake's resting spot. In addition, before wearing, shake out boots and other gear that may invite a scorpion's investigation.

◈ Purify all non-domestic water from all sources before consumption, including water from the Colorado River, creeks, springs, seeps, potholes, and snow accumulation.

◈ There are NO SERVICES between Jacob Lake and Marble Canyon on U.S. Highway 89A in House Rock Valley or between Jacob Lake and the Kaibab Lodge and The Country Store and fueling station on Arizona State Route 67. Verify seasonal service schedules.

◈ Cairns (*Gaelic* for "pile of stones"): Look over your shoulder. One of the best things a hiker can do for himself is to remark a route by setting cairns high enough to be seen over ridgelines and brush and other route obstacles so they are easily detectable on the way out.

In protection position. Rattlesnakes use their strike mechanism as a last form of self-defense. (GRCA 5770)

ENCOUNTERING HOUSE ROCK VALLEY

The Vermilion Cliffs soar above for the California condor, and buffalo roam in the valley below the Henry Mountains. House Rock Valley is a solitary setting in the United States where there still can be found the cliff-lined valley distinguished by its lonely openness and also by its dirt roads lined with micro scenery—birds and butterflies, trees and wildflowers, reptiles and mammals, blue skies and clouds. In the spring, dry creek washes fill with the melting snow from the Kaibab Plateau on the North Rim of the Grand Canyon and rage—*gully washers*—in monsoonal thunderstorms in the summer. This is House Rock Valley.

It is sunrise and discreetly unveiled is a novel day where bands of hunters and gatherers and nomadic tribes left behind confirmation of their presence. In 1776, the Southern Paiute warned the Spanish expedition of Escalante and Dominguez, who were searching for a practical mission route from Santa Fe to the coast of California at Monterey, not to rely on the scantiness of the valley.

The Spaniards, who were *famé-lico*—famished—bartered with the tribe for rabbit meat, grass seeds, and piñon pine nuts to survive. Much later, stagecoach route maps prove the region rugged, avoiding the real problem being the lack of water—for everyone—and the obvious problem being the barrier of the Grand Canyon.

The name "House Rock" was formalized by John Wesley Powell's expedition beginning in 1871. Crew member Frederick Dellenbaugh journaled:

East Rim. Sunrise over the Henry Mountains and Marble Canyon in House Rock Valley.

About sunset we pass two large boulders which had fallen together, forming a rude shelter, under which [Charley] Riggs or someone else had slept, and then jocosely printed above with charcoal words Rock House Hotel.

Land tract. Expansive House Rock Valley between U.S. 89A and the horizon of Saddle Mountain.

Old West. A cattleman's range fence along Forest Development Road 8910 in House Rock Valley seemingly corals the saddle of Saddle Mountain.

Cattle ranching families, such as Levi Stewart and his son-in-law David Udall, established a presence along with stock outfits such as the Canaan Cooperative Stock Company and Van Slack and Thompson, who secured water rights in the North Rim meadows and forests of DeMotte Park's Pleasant Valley initiating the VT brand in the 1870s. Given the rustling environment of the region, the VT brand was simple yet difficult to alter by rustlers. The VT brand was up for sale and purchased in 1896 by Benjamin Saunders and formalized in 1899 as the Grand Canyon Cattle Company.

The "catalo" experiment had its beginnings in 1905 with Edwin Wooley, James T. "Uncle Jim" Owens, and Charles "Buffalo" Jones, and a federal permit to do so on the Kaibab Plateau was granted by 1906. The buffalo arrived by train at Lund, Utah, and were then driven to the North Rim and pastured near Bright Angel Point. The plan ultimately failed due to the poor quality of the new breed. The offspring that the bison-cattle herd produced were smaller than the pure breeds. Field historian Sharlot Hall

Where buffalo roam. Lone bull buffalo, June 24, 1949, in House Rock Valley. The U.S. Game and Fish Department warns not to approach wildlife, including buffalo. (GRCA 1862)

Slower road speeds advised. Cattle line the shoulders of Forest Development Road 8910 in House Rock Valley.

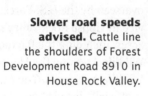

Affectionately known as Uncle Jim. James T. Owens (second from left) with friends on the North Rim, possibly near Bright Angel Spring Meadow, where Uncle Jim maintained a cabin that was built into the Kaibab Limestone. (GRCA 5281)

and her guide Allan Doyle made a circuit by horse and wagon of the Grand Canyon and Arizona Strip in an attempt to retain the strip for Arizona from a Utah annexation. They reported seeing the cattalo herd: *They are smaller than the full bloods, with sharper horns and without beautiful manes.* Hall's and Doyle's excursion in 1911 around the Grand Canyon was a last-ditch but successful effort to save the aft region of Arizona from Utah's annexation attempt. It was due to the lawlessness of the region of the North

Rim and Arizona Strip that Utah made this annexation attempt, in addition to reasons that were geographical. In due course, the bison migrated to and preferred the lower lands of House Rock Valley. Wooley was bought out by Jones, who ultimately sold the herd in 1934 to the U.S. government for $10,000.

Elusive herd. Artist depiction of roaming bison herd, which occupies the 65,000 acres of two wildlife zones in the House Rock Valley. At times, the herd will pass through a breech in the Boundary Line fence and drift into Grand Canyon National Park. (U.S.D.A. Forest Service kiosk section photo)

At present, the buffalo herd is roughly estimated at 400 animals. The Arizona Fish and Game Department manages the herd as wildlife, while the range itself is overseen by the U.S. Forest Service in House Rock Valley's 65,000 acres, including the Raymond Wildlife Area and the House Rock Wildlife Area units. The valley area is officially listed at 60,000 acres, however the rugged regional cliffs to the west of the valley are now considered in the acreage tabulation. The Arizona Game and Fish Department manages a "buffalo fair chase hunt" and issues about 60 permits in the autumn, as determined by the buffalo population. The goal population is 100 head in an attempt to strike a balance with forage supplies. The difficulties rest in that the hunts are unpredictable. The northern Arizona terrain is remote and rugged and the herd has become illusive to the hunter's rifle and will move into the high elevation of the Kaibab National Forest in the winter, favoring such locations as South Canyon over the valley. The herd will also fluctuate in and out of Grand Canyon National Park through breeches in the Boundary Line fence, where hunting is not allowed.

To those who choose the House Rock Valley territory as their entry point to the Nankoweap Trail, the basin may seem barren on either side of this segment of U.S. Highway 89A and farther on Forest Development Road 8910 toward the trailhead of Trail #31. Compared to the forested North Rim alpine regions, to some the valley is lacking, while many find a natural surplus. The profile of Saddle Mountain is obvious even while far afield from U.S. 89A. Arrive equipped with the gear appropriate not only for the trail, but also with the hardware needed for the Forest Development Roads (FDR). Both person and vehicle will need to be prepared to maneuver the intricacies of remote desert and alpine travel.

After departing the comfort of the North Rim region's small northern Arizona towns, it is on to the U.S. Forest Service's Forest Development Roads where the backcountry experience truly begins. There is adventure in reaching any of the Nankoweap trailheads and the ultimate destination, the Colorado River, at the bottom of the canyon. ’

Chalet. Uncle Jim's North Rim cabin entrance in Bright Angel Spring Meadow, along the road to Widforss Point and Point Sublime.

ROADS & TRAILHEADS
WRAPPED IN HISTORY

In 1917, the Kaibab National Forest—Arizona map, issued under USDA Forester Henry Graves, did not illustrate roads to the interior of the House Rock Valley. Beyond pioneering homesteader roads, such as that of the Kane and Buffalo Ranches, specific House Rock Valley roads are now maintained to access, particularly in the winter, the Nankoweap Trail and other interests in the vicinity. By 1962, United States Geological Survey maps included the road from US 89A, designated as Forest Service Roads 1049 branching onto 445, which have now been jointly reassigned as Forest Development Road 8910.

The end of road 445, termed the "old road," was converted into the first 1.5 miles of Trail #31 and is utilized as the beginning section—the approach—to the historic Nankoweap Trail within the Grand Canyon. Today, the "road" is closed to mechanized travel and must be walked, as it is overgrown with brush, encroached on by a juniper and piñon woodland, and beset with rain runoff and snowmelt stream bedding. In some years, this pass is not accessible in the rainy seasons, as FDR 8910 can become impassable due to mud or swollen washes or snow may blanket the road in winter. These conditions will also impact the trail and may surmount the saddle of Saddle Mountain, the location of the National Park Service's Nankoweap Trailhead within Grand Canyon National Park.

When Grand Canyon became a national park in 1919, a trail fragmentation was caused by the new park's centered boundary line within the Kaibab National Forest. The Nankoweap Trail was left within the national park and the Inner Canyon, but outside of the U.S. Forest Service's jurisdiction, and today its approach routes—Trails #31 and Trail #57—are in the Kaibab National Forest.

The Nankoweap Trail's access is unlike any other named route going from rim to river within the national park's boundaries because there is no direct mechanized route to the National Park Service's designated trailhead within Grand Canyon National Park. Its original trail section was near Point Imperial on Saddle Mountain, where John Wesley Powell and Charles Doolittle Walcott first improved upon the "old Indian trail" in the autumn of 1882. This original trail-

Road schematics. (USGS-Hefley)

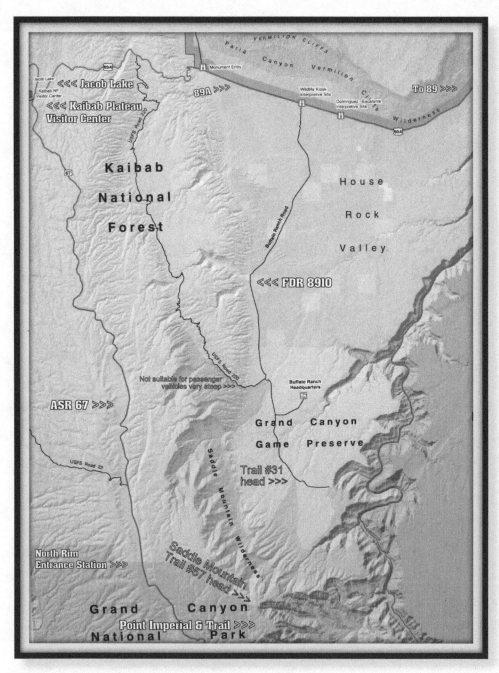

Regional road layout. USDA Forest Service kiosk section photo. (USDA-Hefley)

head location near Point Imperial is validated because Powell wrote that, once he left Walcott and his assistants to do geologic work in the Nankoweap Basin in the canyon over the winter, they would become "blocked" by the North Rim's accumulation of snow—snowed in—"below the summit of the Plateau."

In their 1934 *Grand Canyon Nature Notes*, the Grand Canyon Natural History Association (now Grand Canyon Association) printed Walter Wagner's topological (simplified) map of the Nankoweap Valley illustrating the Point Imperial trailhead. The Kane Ranch road and workings were established circa 1892, ten years after Powell and Walcott improved the Indian path into the Nankoweap Trail. The Kane Ranch and Buffalo Ranch Road, which accesses the House Rock Valley trailhead today, are maintained by the U.S. Forest Service as FDR 8910.

The *Boundary Ridge* notation on USGS maps defines the former definite border line of Grand Canyon National Park with Marble Canyon National Monument. In 1975, President Gerald Ford reset and opened the park boundaries at the Colorado River and along the Marble Canyon rim with the incorporation of the Marble Canyon National Monument and the Grand Canyon National Park. Ford authorized a contiguous Grand Canyon National Park. This expansion improved environmental protection for Marble Canyon by giving it national park status. Found at the Marble Canyon and Grand Canyon transition below Barbenceta Butte is the Colorado River and the end of the Nankoweap Trail.

Accessing the Nankoweap Approach Roads

CAUTION: Watch for animals crossing all highways and roads. Where fencing does appear, it may be unable to contain the enthusiastic animals for which it is intended.

U.S. Highway 89A (Alternate) is termed an auxiliary highway to U.S. Highway 89 and was the mainline highway until the construction of Glen Canyon Dam. In 1960, U.S. Highway 89 was rerouted to a more northerly direction to access the dam site. U.S. Highway 89 crosses its own bridge in front of the face of the dam, and is the same design as the Navajo Bridges. This is the last remaining section of Glen Canyon that is not inundated by the waters of Lake Powell. From the junction of U.S. Highways 89 and 89A, the highway travels in a westerly direction passing over the modern Navajo Bridge, past the turnoff for Lees Ferry, and continues into the elevation of the Kaibab Plateau at Jacob Lake. From Jacob Lake, Highway 89A continues to Fredonia, Arizona, and to the Utah highway segment at Kanab (once commissioned as Utah State Route 11).

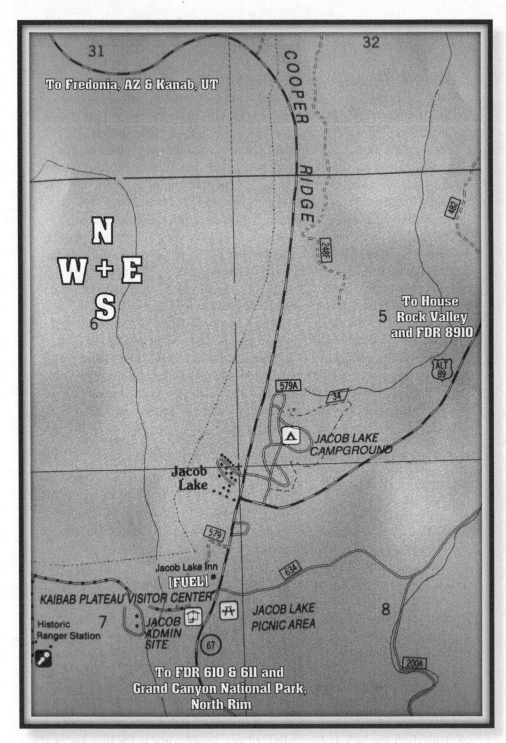

Outpost. Jacob Lake at U.S. 89A and Arizona State Route 67. (USGS-Hefley)

Roadside marker. Entrance sign located between Mileposts 559 and 560 along U.S. 89A at Forest Development Road 8910.
Foreground: eight-inch tall fire ant hill.

The kiosk. Stop here to gain an overview and possible current postings for House Rock Valley. Notice the road entrance marker in the background where the roadbed of U.S. 89A is recessed below the shrub-line and just out of view.

Arizona State Route 67 was once a "cattleman's road" that was re-aligned about .8-mile to the east to its present location and is approximately 31 miles long from the north at the junction of U.S. Highway 89A at Jacob Lake to Grand Canyon National Park's North Rim Entrance Station. This 31-mile section is owned and maintained by the Arizona Department of Transportation.

Once inside the national park, from the entrance station to the terminus at Grand Canyon Lodge at Bright Angel Point, the remaining 12.5 miles of road is maintained by the National Park Service and considered the Grand Canyon Highway section, but commonly called Highway 67.

The road was built in the 1920s and improved throughout the 1930s. Gravel was added in 1935, in 1938 the road was paved, and in 1941 the road received its designation number. In 1985, the road, while retaining its state route number, was also designated as the Kaibab Plateau–North Rim Parkway Scenic Highway.

Jacob Lake Inn is located at the junction of U.S. Highway 89A and Arizona State Route 67 on Cooper Ridge, and can be considered by all travelers to be the nearest outpost of re-supply, as it remains open year-round. At present, the fueling station remains electronically operable after the inn services close in the evening and before reopening in the morning.

The next services are located 30 miles north on U.S. Highway 89A in Fredonia, Arizona, and 7 miles farther in Kanab, Utah. In these small towns, patron hours of operation may vary seasonally and with the weather.

As a solo hiker and group hike leader, driving the Grand Canyon's back area roads to trailheads for more than three decades, I was glad to have and utilized more than one of the listed items, including extra food and water, air compressor, vehicle fluids, jack, spare tire, toolbox items, vehicle water pump, fuse, headlamp, and jumper cables (to start another vehicle). I also learned that it is a good idea to spray tires with bug spray to detour ants from climbing up into a vehicle that will be parked on the forest floor for an extended period.

Travel with a full fuel tank whenever possible. Because this is a remote region of the United States, goods and services are sometimes delayed usually due to inclement weather and the inability to resupply. The drive in and out of House Rock Valley is a classic example, as services are distant and located back at Jacob Lake, Arizona, and Kanab, Utah, or easterly at Page, Arizona, and farther southeasterly at Cameron, Arizona.

Due to administrative changes to USDA Forest Service roads from "Forest Road" to "Forest Service Road" to "Forest Development Road," some road numbers have changed. At present, be aware that the Forest Service Road 445 from 89A at House Rock Valley is now Forest Development Road 8910 and is displayed as such only on some revised maps, while others do not show the modification.

Grand Canyon Forest Development Road Travel

The U.S. Forest Service performs a complete maintenance schedule of the back area roads, however, the roads are still naturally rocky and washouts can occur without notice immediately after a maintenance schedule is performed. In the upper elevations, trees will also fall across roads blocking either the entrance— or exit—from a back area trail. I highly recommend a high ground clearance vehicle. This is a remote region of the United States where services are not established. Consider bringing the following:

◈ Food and water for before, during, and after the hike. Have enough water for domestic activities and extra nonperishable food to endure an extended stay due to a variety of unexpected delays, such as a road blocked by a fallen tree.

◈ Camp gear, beyond that of the backpack's capacity, in the event of a delay on the canyon rim.

◈ Extra vehicle parts such as two spare tires, jumper cables, headlamp, vehicle battery, water pump, starter, alternator, belt(s), wiper blades, fuse kit, radiator "stop leak," and other vehicle parts that can be changed out in the field. In the event of vehicle failure, even if a vehicle can "make it" to the nearest rural community where a mechanic is present, vehicle parts may still be as far away as Flagstaff, Arizona, or Salt Lake City, Utah.

◈ Basic toolbox: crescent wrench (small & medium), hammer, open end wrench set, screw drivers (standard & Phillips), socket set, pliers (standard, needle nose, channel lock), vice grip, utility knife, variety of nuts & bolts, electrical & duct tape, bailing wire & cable "zip" ties, bungee cords, small axe (hatchet), bow saw, leather gloves.

◈ Tow rope and hand operated "come-along" winch.

◈ X-style lug wrench (provides leverage and even torque on lug nuts).

◈ Flat tire repair kit to include "plug" and "spray" style patching kits.

◈ Compact portable air compressor, spotlight—both vehicle cigarette lighter outlet powered.

◈ Jeep jack or compact floor jack and 2 short planks as a jack rest. Most manufacturers' jacks will not have the "reach" or stability on uneven and sloped surfaces of the Forest Development Roads.

Rocky road with loam soil on top. My high ground clearance vehicle near the end of Forest Development Road 610 approaching the Saddle Mountain's trailhead for Trail #57.

Draw. Wash crossings such as this one on FDR 8910 can become vehicle-deep with raging water during summer monsoons.

◈ Snow chains for icy and muddy roads.

◈ Extra fuel & motor oil. Travel with a full vehicle fuel tank whenever possible.

◈ Emergency 12-hour snap-light "light-stick."

◈ Spare door/ignition key kept on person.

Fire plume. Lightning strike-caused forest fires on the Kaibab Plateau may also cause a travel setback on the Forest Development Roads (FDR). It's a good idea to carry an abundance of drinking water, food, and equipment to handle such delays as this, or downed trees that may also block a road. The photo was taken from the shoulder of Arizona State Route 389 near Fredonia, Arizona, looking across the Arizona Strip toward the Toroweap "Sub District," where the Grand Canyon is on the opposite side of the horizon.

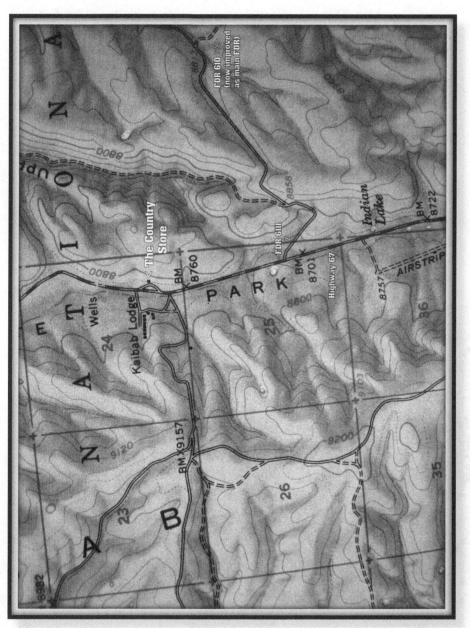

Road layout. Arizona State Route 67 at FDR 611. (USGS-Hefley)

Rim Camp Equipment

The equipment listed below is *essential* for coping with North Rim (9,000-foot elevation) and South Rim (7,500-foot elevation) merging desert-alpine weather systems.

- Tent (at least a 3-season) and tent ground sheet.
- Easy up–style shelter.
- Sleeping bag.
- Lantern with extra fuel or batteries and mantles if necessary.
- Emergency radio with weather band.
- Binoculars.
- Rope & bungee cords.
- Tarps and extra tent stakes.
- Extra clothing & blankets.
- Camp stove.
- Extra matches & fire starter (paste).
- Cook set, utensils, can opener, scissors, aluminum foil, paper towels, dish soap, Ziploc bags.
- Food: canned and dry goods.
- Water.
- Trash bags.
- Toilet paper & hand sanitizer.
- Work gloves.
- Firewood.

High above. At-large rim camp in the Kaibab National Forest. House Rock Valley and Marble Canyon below in the vicinity of FDR 8910 and Trail #31. Notice the wind-block backing built into the fire ring.

Junction. Paved apron of FDR 611 transitions to dirt and rocks at Arizona State Route 67.

Road splits. The division of FDR 611 at the beginning of FDR 610. FDR 610 was once a secondary route and is still shown as such on USGS maps. However, the 610 road has been reworked into the primary travel route to Saddle Mountain and the road nearer to the North Rim Entrance Station that shows as a primary travel route is presently closed to mechanized travel.

Posted. Limit forest fires to natural causes.

THE NANKOWEAP TRAILHEADS

Introduction

OVERVIEW: There is one contiguous Kaibab National Forest trail system that makes a connection to the Inner Canyon Nankoweap Trail. These are joint use Trail #31 and Trail #57. Trails #31 & #57 are designated as "pack trails" and are not expected to be more than 40 inches wide.

The United States Department of Agriculture's U.S. Forest Service Trails #31 and #57 in the Kaibab National Forest, in their entirety, are a combined 6.5 miles long between their two trailheads at Saddle Mountain (Trail #57) and House Rock Valley (Trail #31) to the Kaibab monocline's rendezvous in the steep canyons and white cliffs where the official Nankoweap Trail's trailhead is met on the ridgeline of Saddle Mountain. The Nankoweap Trail is intercepted at about the halfway point along this combined U.S. Forest Service trail system.

National Park Service trailhead. The official Nankoweap Trailhead located at the rendezvous with Trail #57 in the saddle of Saddle Mountain.

National Forest trailhead. Trail #31 at the end of FDR 8910 in House Rock Valley.

Access: Three Trailheads

Access to all three trailheads starts at Jacob Lake, Arizona, located at the junction of U.S. Highway 89A (Alternate) and Arizona State Route 67.

1. House Rock Valley: The Nankoweap Trail is **14.5 miles** long from House Rock Valley (Trail #31 to Trail #57 to Nankoweap Trail). The head of Trail #31 is at the apex of Forest Development Road 8910. The slight cul-de-sac at the road's apex in House Rock Valley creates a small parking area.

2. Saddle Mountain: The Nankoweap Trail is **14 miles** long from Saddle Mountain (Trail #57 to Nankoweap Trail). Trail #57 on Saddle Mountain, near Point Imperial, curves down into the saddle of Saddle Mountain, the location of the Inner Canyon Nankoweap Trail, and continues to the Trail #31 junction in House Rock Valley.

3. Point Imperial Trail: The Nankoweap Trail is **16.2 miles** long from Point Imperial (Point Imperial Trail to Forest Development Road 610 to the beginning of Trail #57 on Saddle Mountain to Nankoweap Trail).

Nankoweap Trail System

(USGS-Hefley)

National Forest trailhead. Trail #57, called the Nankoweap Trail, is the historic route section through the Kaibab National Forest between the end of FDR 610 on Saddle Mountain and the official National Park Service trailhead. The upper route was dissected by administrative changes to the region, which realigned the official NPS trailhead farther to the east. However, hikers that start at Point Imperial in Grand Canyon National Park transition into the Kaibab National Forest on FDR 610, then onto the Trail #57 section, and then transition back into the Grand Canyon National Park at the now official trailhead site.

Trail to Forest Development Road transition. Out of the brush of the Point Imperial Trail and onto FDR 610 near the Saddle Mountain Trail #57. The photo was taken from FDR 610.

All these beginnings rendezvous the hiker at the Trail #57's approximate halfway point at the North Rim in the saddle below the "saddle horn" of Saddle Mountain and intercept the Inner Canyon Nankoweap Trail at the Kaibab National Forest and the Grand Canyon National Park Boundary Line fence, called "Boundary Ridge," which was once the easternmost border of Grand Canyon National Park. The national park boundary line expanded northeasterly to include Marble Canyon.

From any of the three trailheads, the hike seemingly hasn't quite started. The trails leading from any trailhead are difficult overture approaches and will start the fatigue process in a hiker before the hike on the non-maintained Inner Canyon Nankoweap Trail has started—and has ended. The most challenging start-to-finish is from Point Imperial, which is the longest sectional hike. On return to the established National Park Service's designated trailhead, there can be a feeling of great accomplishment. For others, it's a feeling of relief. However, the hike really has not ended as each respective approach trail section remains to be walked, in reverse, to the parking areas. The defining moment is in the finish or last leg of the hike and, some-times, the last legs of the hiker.

Selecting a Trailhead

CAUTION: Rain and snow and ice on the Nankoweap Trail's upper ledge-ways compound the danger rating. Proper winter gear, skill, and discernment will be necessary. Carry shoe traction such as crampons or similar devices. On the con-trary, the south-facing Nankoweap Trail is not recommended as a summer hike as temperatures elevate and there is little chance for shade.

> **Hiking from, and back to, the Saddle Mountain
> and Point Imperial trailheads is physically
> more demanding than hiking from, and back to,
> the House Rock Valley trailhead.**

One can start in the elevation of Saddle Mountain on Trail #57 in the spring through autumn, or in the lower-lands of House Rock Valley on Trail #31 almost year around. However, in the dead of most winters, the Point Imperial Trail and Trail #57 on Saddle Mountain may not be desirable or accessible due to the North Rim's 200 inches of expected snow accumulation and, in general terms,

Forest Service Road classic. Cattleguards replaced the barbed wire stretch-gates on main Forest Development Roads, but gates are still used on many other roads. Range fences, gates, and guards protect the land by the opening and closing of pastures for periods of rest from grazing.

the closing of Grand Canyon, North Rim, region roads and services. The North Rim technically stays open year-round with very limited services to those who cross-country ski or snowshoe to the rim. It is up to the individual to clarify what is open or closed.

A winter hike scenario from the Trail #57 trailhead on Saddle Mountain: suppose access is available and not already blocked by snow on Forest Service Roads 611 and 610 at the start of a hike. However, while in the canyon, a massive storm front moves in and blankets the upper elevations of the North Rim with snow. Therefore, House Rock Valley should be the trailhead of choice in the winter.

Still, the valley access may not provide access due to an accumulation of snow, either at the trailhead or on Saddle Mountain, or both. Chances are better that the hiking plan may not be foiled at the start when beginning from House Rock Valley in the winter. On return, the Saddle Mountain section of Trail #57 brings the hiker up and over the ridges of the Kaibab monocline near its highest elevation, and along Boundary Ridge several times until making a final ascent to the parking area.

In their own ways, the Forest Service trailheads are striking. Saddle Mountain and Point Imperial are impressive for their conifers, aspens, maples, and

House Rock Valley entry. FDR 8910 closing in on the trailhead for Trail #31.

transitional summits. House Rock Valley is arresting for its piñon and juniper woodland, yellow broom snakeweed, and seemingly measureless open range loneliness. The House Rock Valley section-grade is predominantly downhill to the parking area with an incline out of a valley at the end.

Accessing the Trailheads

COLORADO RIVER: ELEVATION 2,802 feet at the confluence of the Colorado River and Nankoweap Creek. (USGS map *Nankoweap Mesa Quadrangle* 7.5 Minute Series [Topographic])

Saddle Mountain Trail

(a.k.a. U.S. Forest Service Trail #57 Nankoweap Trail)
Elevation: 8,800 feet at the Saddle Mountain Wilderness
Map needed: USGS map Nankoweap Quadrangle 15 Minute Series (Topographic).
Distance: 3 miles to the Nankoweap Trail

Travel south on Arizona State Route 67 from Jacob Lake, Arizona, toward Grand Canyon's North Rim for 27.5 miles and toward the DeMotte Park Campground entrance. Pass the DeMotte Park Campground entrance road and travel

Vear left. Trail #57 just below the trailhead on Saddle Mountain at the end of FDR 610 descends to the northeast (left) while a dead-end trail ascends to overlook the Nankoweap Basin.

.6 mile and turn east (left) onto Forest Development Road 611. Travel 1.4 miles and turn south (right) onto Forest Development Road 610. (At the time of this printing, the Kaibab National Forest maintains a permanent lavatory structure 6 miles from highway 67). The road travels through Upper North Canyon and continues for 12.3 miles to the cul-de-sac at the end of the road and the trailhead site. The North Kaibab Ranger District maintains the two off-highway roads in a manner suitable for passenger cars. However, the roads are very rocky, making them best suited to high ground clearance vehicles. NO SERVICES.

The trailhead is in the southeast corner of the parking area and is well marked with a Kaibab National Forest placard. The trail starts in the old-growth forest of ponderosa pine, aspen, and maple. In approximately 100 paces the trail forks. Stay to the left as the right fork deadends on top of this portion of Saddle Mountain. A Kaibab National Forest trail stake marking the correct way is present.

The left fork descends rapidly and then ascends rapidly up and over the hillocks and ridges, then descends through manzanita and locust onto an open grassy meadow before descending very steep through the conifer forest to the terraces of Supai Sandstone at the National Park Service official trailhead site.

<<<Trail #57 on Saddle Mountain

On top. Trail #57 in the pine, aspen, and maple on Saddle Mountain.

Along the way, the trail is sufficiently marked with cairns.

Note: The North Kaibab Ranger District documents Trail #57 as the "Nankoweap Trail #57" but is commonly called Trail #57. With some general realignment, this is the original Powell-Walcott section.

Seasonally on Saddle Mountain: Water may be possible from snow accumulation only. This method of water capture is an extreme practice and should only be attempted by highly experienced Grand Canyon hikers—those who are frequently out in canyon country and understand the risk of a lack of water. Carry a sufficient amount of water and water containers in the first place.

Point Imperial Trail

(General extension of Trail #57)
Elevation: 8,803 feet at Grand Canyon National Park.
Map Needed: USGS map Nankoweap Quadrangle 15 Minute Series
    (Topographic)
Distance: 5.2 miles to the official NPS Inner Canyon Nankoweap Trail

Travel south from Jacob Lake on Arizona State Route 67 and enter Grand Canyon National Park (fee required at the North Rim Entrance Station). From the North Rim Entrance Station, travel 9.7 miles to the Cape Royal Road and turn east (left). Travel 5.4 miles to the Y in the road and branch off northerly (left) and travel 3 miles to Point Imperial. At this road junction is the developing Bright Angel Canyon at Neal Spring (named for

To Point Imperial. The Cape Royal Road on the North Rim at Neal Spring.

Time warp. At the elevation of 8,803 feet from the Point Imperial Trail, the Nankoweap Trail is invisible to the naked eye as it is in repose on the geologically distorted Kaibab Monocline.

cattleman William Neal [1849–1936]), the headwater source of Bright Angel Creek. **Point Imperial parking** is allowed by designation on the Backcountry Use Permit at the time of application. Except for a lavatory, there are NO SERVICES at Point Imperial.

The Point Imperial Trail is on the easterly side of the parking area. Providing a tie-in to Trail #57, the Point Imperial Trail follows the rim region for 2 miles traveling a formerly designated fire road that links Point Imperial to Forest Development Road 610 at the Grand Canyon National Park–Kaibab National Forest Boundary Line fence. From the gate at the boundary line fence, it is another .2 mile to the trailhead of Trail #57 on Saddle Mountain.

The hike along the North Rim reveals the Grand Canyon's Nankoweap Basin to the south and to the north the depression in the land that forms the headcanyon of Bright Angel Creek. The burn area is the result of the Outlet Fire in April of 2000. (A misnomer on some maps, the Point Imperial Trail should not be mistaken for the southwesterly Ken Patrick Trail, which is at the opposite end of the parking area and links Point Imperial with the North Kaibab Trail parking area.)

House Rock Valley Trail

(Saddle Mountain Trail #31 to the U.S. Forest Service Section Nankoweap
   Trail #57)
Elevation 6,760 feet at the Buffalo Ranch Road
Map Needed: USGS map Nankoweap Quadrangle 15 Minute Series
   (Topographic)
Distance: 3.5 miles to the Nankoweap Trail

The House Rock Valley, from Trail #31, provides access to Trail #57 in the Kaibab National Forest and the Nankoweap Trail in Grand Canyon National Park during the winter when snow accumulation inhibits practical access to and from Saddle Mountain. Year around, the House Rock Valley entry is the most commonly used approach. NO SERVICES.

Travel easterly from Jacob Lake on U.S. Highway 89A (Alternate) in House Rock Valley. Turn south on FDR 8910 (formerly Forest Service Road 445) where it T's in between mileposts 559 and 560. An information kiosk of the Buffalo Ranch marks the pull-in area. Travel through House Rock Valley for 27.5 miles, crossing over many cattle guards and through 20 significant dry washes to the designated trailhead parking area. The parking area comfortably holds just a few vehicles. The North Kaibab Ranger District maintains FDR 8910 in a manner that may be "suitable for passenger cars." However, the road is rocky and crosses

The "ravine." Saddle Canyon, called the ravine section, and House Rock Valley from Trail #57 on Saddle Mountain.

many large washes that become active during rain or snowmelt conditions stemming from the North Rim, making the roads best suited to high ground clearance vehicles. Some of the more notable washes driven across along the way to the parking area include those which develop into major side canyons within Grand Canyon National Park's Marble Canyon at a level with the Colorado River: North Canyon Wash (river mile 20.5), and Fence and Wildcat Canyons that culminate with South Canyon (river mile 31.7).

Once on Trail #57, the "ravine" that is traversed before the long climb to the high country of Saddle Mountain is Saddle Canyon, where, at river level in Marble Canyon, the Triple Alcoves formation is located.

From the parking area at the apex of the turnout, the trailhead for Trail #31 is visible and marked with a formal Kaibab National Forest placard. The trail descends into a small wash and continues by following the "old road" as it ascends through a juniper and piñon pine forest. Marble Canyon at Eminence Break can be seen as you gain in elevation past the ravine, which is the head drainage of Saddle Canyon stemming from Saddle Mountain. The trail sharply ascends to Saddle Mountain and the Nankoweap Trail at Grand Canyon National Park.

Winter in the summer. The North Rim Entrance Station after a six-inch snow fall and melt-off in July, 2011. It is prudent to bring a broad gear selection to either rim for final weather and gear assessment prior to entering the canyon and to survive possible delays on the rim.

Most people site Trail #57 as the access trailhead in and from House Rock Valley. However, it is Trail # 31, the Saddle Mountain Trail, which leads off from the parking area and then junctions with Trail #57 in approximately 1 mile. From the junction, the Saddle Mountain Trail #31 continues to the east to access the eastern tip of Boundary Ridge and dead-ends.

Back at the junction, Trail #57 (designated as the Kaibab National Forest's section of the Nankoweap Trail) continues northwesterly for 2.5 miles to the junction with the Nankoweap Trail proper, nestled within the saddle of Saddle Mountain at the Kaibab National Forest–Grand Canyon National Park Boundary Line. This is the rendezvous site.

The Nankoweap Trail proper continues into the canyon and Trail #57 makes an arch westerly away and out of the saddle and continues to the higher elevations at the parking areas for the Trail #57 trailhead on Saddle Mountain and the Point Imperial trailhead (see map on page 36).

Seasonally on the House Rock Valley trails: During periods of sufficient rain, snowmelt, and snow, it is possible to renew drinking water en route. These water sources are NOT reliable. Carry a sufficient amount water and water containers from the start in the event ravines and potholes are dry. This method of water capture is an extreme practice and should only be attempted by highly experienced Grand Canyon hikers—those who are frequently out in canyon country and understand the risks.

The Nankoweap is a great trail. The difficulty of the trail depends on how it is approached. The National Park Service is trying to maintain the wilderness character—and the wilderness is clearly having no problem. No shortage of trees and boulders falling from Saddle Mountain.

—Steve Bridgehouse,
Grand Canyon National Park

One gallon treatment. Purifying water at Nankoweap Creek.

THE NANKOWEAP TRAIL

Grand Canyon National Park Trailhead Elevation 7,640 feet
- ❖ **Purify all water.**
- ❖ **Perennial Water Sources:** ONLY Nankoweap Creek and the Colorado River.
- ❖ **Ephemeral (Seasonal) Water Source:** Marion Point Seep may be located under a ledge shortly after where the route passes Marion Point.
- ❖ **Cache 4 quarts of water per person on Tilted Mesa on the way in for use on the way out. Capture, purify, and carry at least 4 more quarts of water per person at Nankoweap Creek for the way out. Once Nankoweap Creek is left behind, the distance to the North Rim is waterless. The word cache, pronounced *cash*, is from the French *cacher* meaning "to hide." Label all caches with name and date. The National Park Service requires that all caches and cache containers are to be removed on the return to the rim.**

Mt Hayden, July. Grand Canyon weather extreme; Nankoweap Basin below the clouds.

Mt. Hayden, October. Weather role reversal; Nankoweap Basin in the background.

Of the more than twenty named trails and routes in Grand Canyon National Park, only one—the Nankoweap Trail—respectfully has a nickname: *Nank*. The unmaintained Nankoweap Trail in its entirety is in Grand Canyon National Park's Use Area called AE9 and should not be mistaken for Trail #31 leading out of House Rock Valley and Trail #57 leading off of Saddle Mountain to the National Park Service dedicated trailhead at the Boundary Line fence at Boundary Ridge. While Trail #31 and Trail #57 and the Nankoweap Trail are separate entities, total mileage postings are all-inclusive because the Inner Canyon Nankoweap Trail cannot be accessed by mechanized travel.

Like some of Grand Canyon's other remote use areas, such as the South Rim's Tanner Trail (the Nankoweap Trail's counterpart) located below the Indian Watchtower at Desert View, the Nankoweap Trail is predominantly situated below the established, but isolated, Point Imperial. Be that as it may, hiker assistance is absent.

Nankoweap Trail Hiking Strategies

All strategies require sufficient water, food, and equipment per person per day to accomplish either plan listed below. The National Park Service advises not to attempt a rim-to-river trip in a single day on the treacherous Nankoweap Trail.

For safety, walking speed should be unhurried. When stopping to rest or make adjustments, stop where the route widens sufficiently to provide a "nesting" area.

Plan 1: Three days one-way. *Day One:* Trailhead to Kaibab National Forest and Grand Canyon National Park Boundary. No Permit required to camp in the national forest. *Day Two:* the official commencement and first day of the Backcountry Use Permit issued by the National Park Service: Hike from the Boundary Line to Tilted Mesa. *Day Three:* Tilted Mesa to Nankoweap Creek and the Colorado River.

September, 2012. From the South Rim at Navajo Point toward the North Rim. Saddle Mountain makes up the horizon above Nankoweap Basin.

April, 2012. From the South Rim at Desert View toward the North Rim. Nankoweap Basin on the horizon behind and under the storm system.

Plan 2: Two days one-way. *Day One:* Trailhead to Tilted Mesa. *Day Two:* Tilted Mesa to Nankoweap Creek and the Colorado River.

Nankoweap Trail Inner Canyon Sections

The trail sections are reached after the chosen approach trailhead and segment has been walked. The following sections are within the Inner Canyon of Grand Canyon National Park. Section mileages are approximates due to trail washouts that require route reconfigurations.

Section 1: Switchback descent

Distance: approximately 100 feet
Geologic Formation: Supai Sandstone

As a hiker enters the canyon, the trail turns south and descends through the uppermost Supai Sandstone cliffs called the Esplanade and reaches the start of the ledge-way section between Seiber (Sieber) and Marion Points.

Grand Canyon National Park's USE AREA CODE AE9

The Nankoweap Trail is in Grand Canyon National Park's Use Area AE9. The code broken down, "A" stands for the north side of the Colorado River, "E" stands for the fifth section west of Lees Ferry (Grand Canyon's eastern terminus with Glen Canyon), and "9" stands for "At Large" the type of overnight camping allowed. Codes beginning with the letter "B" designate use areas on the south side of the Colorado River. A code beginning with "C" designates Corridor use areas, such as the Bright Angel Campground, even though the site is on the north side of the river.

Nankoweap region overview. (USGS-Hefley)

Hundred-mile view. Nankoweap Basin from Point Imperial. Mt. Hayden is just out of view (right).

Saddle horn turned gun site. On the trail, land formations, such as the saddle horn of Saddle Mountain, become monitors of progress in and out of the canyon.

Ledge-ways. Inner Canyon Nankoweap Trail near Marion Point.

Slow going. The "Scary Spot." The famous, or infamous, segment within the ledge-way section. The route by map and the route by topography may look level from Point Imperial, however, the route goes up, over, around, and undulates.

Lost in space: From the Scary Spot looking some 1,000 feet down into the unnamed side canyon below Marion Point. The elevation varies by the hundreds of feet and was referenced here using the USGS map Nankoweap Quadrangle, 15 Minute Series. (See above photo.)

<<<The route passes between the tree and the cliff

On edge. On-trail tight-tolerances throughout the Nankoweap Trail.

Navajo Indian Reservation

Nankoweap Mesa

Tilted Mesa

Route finding. Passing from ledge-ways to the top of Tilted Mesa.

Transition. A view up-trail ramping onto Tilted Mesa.

Windbreak. Sandstone and piñon form a windscreen camp on Tilted Mesa.

Section 2: Traverse from the switchbacks to Marion Point and Tilted Mesa

Distance: 5 miles
Geologic Formation: Supai Sandstone

Once below the switchbacks, the route begins an expansive traverse contouring the exposed approximately 1,000-foot high ledge-ways on the Esplanade Formation directly below Saddle Mountain's Boundary Ridge. A small seep (usually active in the spring when the North Rim's snowmelt supercharges most ephemeral springs) occurs under a ledge immediately around the sharp turn away from the Marion Point Formation. This spring should NOT be relied upon.

There are a few small campsites at Marion Point. To start reducing pack weight, consider depositing half of your water cache at Marion Point. From Marion Point, the elevated traversing route continues in an undulating fashion over dips and rises and over boulders and trees that have fallen from Saddle Mountain. Ultimately, the traverse gives way to the gradual sloping ridgeline descent onto Tilted Mesa above Little Nankoweap Canyon.

The lead-off on Tilted Mesa is marked by two very large cairns on either

Up and away. The loftiness of the Nankoweap Trail is made real by the cairn set marking the way down the ridges and slopes of Tilted Mesa. Unlike any other named route in Grand Canyon National Park, the elevation losses and gains between the start of the hike and Tilted Mesa seem almost negligible, as gauged by the height relationship with Mt. Hayden and Point Imperial on the horizon.

The route leading down Tilted Mesa

Safety camp. On the way in, it's prudent to ration water and camp on Tilted Mesa so as to start on "fresh legs" the next day.

side of a 3-foot wide notch. The route negotiates a few steep ledge descents by using two trees and their branches for handholds. The route descends the northerly slope of Tilted Mesa.

On Tilted Mesa, consider reducing pack weight again by depositing the remaining water cache and, in a rodent-proof container, consider caching food items that will be consumed at Tilted Mesa on the return and on the remaining return hike to the North Rim. There are several nice campsites on Tilted Mesa that are a strategic fit for rest and recuperation for either the way in or the way out of the canyon. It is advisable to use these sites to conserve the body. Below Tilted Mesa, the way is VERY STEEP.

Section 3: Tilted Mesa descent to the Tapeats Sandstone and Nankoweap Creek

Distance: 3 miles
Geologic Formations: Redwall Limestone transitioning to Bright Angel Shale and Tapeats Sandstone

Below and on the talus slopes of Tilted Mesa, the route continues in deteriorated, unpronounced switchback slalom-style segments. The route in the upper

Redwall is obvious and moderately well constructed. Where it is gravelly, the rocks are angular and large enough to stabilize under the foot. The route deteriorates when it makes several wayward traverses, and then descends straight down a drifting ridge of yellowish shale.

At the base of this distinctive talus slope, the route turns back to the northwest and onto a plunging ridge of semi-stable conglomerate boulder debris. The trail down this ridge is extremely steep and abrupt. When the route approaches a large colorful geologic knob, it then turns back to the southeast onto another slender and loose traverse through Bright Angel Shale.

Below the Bright Angel Shale, the route continues in the contours of the mesa apron and then onto the slopes and terraces of the Tapeats Sandstone and

Tree hand-holds below Tilted Mesa

Hand-hold. Descent off Tilted Mesa, for a time, is made with the aid of piñon branches. Throughout any canyoneering experience, test the strength of handholds before bearing weight.

Little Colorado River Gorge

Temple Butte

Chuar Butte

Gunther Castle

Nankoweap Mesa

<<<The route section below Tilted Mesa

<<<Nankoweap Creek

Be mindful. Below Tilted Mesa, the real descent is about to begin. In canyoneering, what goes down must come up.

on to Nankoweap Creek. Marking the route transition into and out of the Nankoweap Creek bed, there is a cottonwood tree with a gnarled trunk and, creek washouts permitting, two large cairns (one on top of a boulder and one located immediately downstream of the first).

Section 4: Nankoweap Creek to the Colorado River

Distance: 3 miles
Geologic Formation: Cardenas Basalt

The creek branches off from itself frequently then reconvenes with itself until it ultimately makes its confluence with the Colorado River at a boatman's river mile 52.5 from Lees Ferry. The creek route, located within the confines of Nankoweap Canyon, is straightforward following the water grade over cobblestones except where one or more of the creek's spillways are encountered, requiring "boulder hopping." The route will change from season to season as rain and snowmelt from the North Rim may supercharge the creek's volume, altering the condition of the creek bed.

Near the confluence of the creek with the river, an established, well-marked trail comes in from the south. The trail continues in a rise traveling to the significant beaches of the Colorado River (at this point, flowing from a northerly direction) and the Nankoweap Ruin located approximately 500 feet above river level in the Nankoweap Mesa's northeast corner facing the river. The canyon wall on the opposite side of the river is the Desert Facade and region of the Navajo Indian Reservation of the Diné (meaning "the People") at Blue Moon Bench. This is the Nankoweap Creek Delta at the Lower Marble Canyon–Grand Canyon transition zone at the Colorado River.

From the rise, the northerly view is of the lower reaches and confines of Barbenceta Butte, named after the Navajo chief who aided John Wesley Powell's second expedition in 1871. The unnamed distant geologic knob is at an elevation of 4,823 feet. The horizon through the northerly river corridor is the Sase Nasket formation (from the Navajo, variably meaning "petrified sand dunes").

Colorado River camp: Occupy any open beach site. Note that the beaches upstream from the confluence of the river and Nankoweap Creek near Little Nankoweap Creek will offer solitude from possible river parties who camp at-large downstream.

Relief. The first view of Nankoweap Creek from the Tapeats Formation.

The door. Primary cairn set and gnarled cottonwood tree marking the way in and out of the Nankoweap Creek bed.

Picking out the creek route. View upstream shortly after leaving the route transition from the Tapeats Formation to the Nankoweap Creek bed. On the horizon is the North Rim between Point Imperial and Vista Encantadora (formerly Vista Encantada, meaning enchanted view—in 1941 Grand Canyon National Park Superintendent, Harold C. Bryant, changed the name to Vista Encantadora, meaning enchanting view).

Quicksand. Foot-deep wet basalt in Nankoweap Canyon between Barbenceta Butte and lower Nankoweap Mesa (right side).

Old-fashioned trouble shooting. The creek bed will change from year to year as flash floods and snow melt move debris to river level. When hiking creek beds, keep a sharp ear for coursing thundering water. In some parts of Grand Canyon, it could be raining in Utah with the end result in Arizona's Grand Canyon. Here, the route is to the left over the top of the downed cottonwood tree.

It's how we roll. Boulder hopping to the left of the spillway. Trekking poles are a key addition to Grand Canyon hiking gear. Saving spills in the moment and the knees over time, trekking poles are like having 4-wheel drive.

The end of the Nankoweap Trail near river level. *The colors are such ... that the light seems to glow or shine out of the rock rather than to be reflected from it.*—Clarence Dutton, 1880.

INNER CANYON PROVISIONS

Appetites tend to diminish when hiking in hot climates. Eat to remain energized. Foods need to be appetizing to promote frequent eating, nutritious to keep energy levels up, and salty to reduce the risk of a condition called *hyponatremia* (See *First Aid Kit*)

Use a steel mesh bag or cookie tin to keep animals out of your food caches. Repackage foods that have bulky containers into one-quart size ziplock freezer bags. Once empty, ziplock bags become utility ware. Grand Canyon backpacking foods tend to revolve around snacks that are highly desirable and are high in nutrition, high in calories, and salty. Eating frequently maintains energy and electrolyte levels over the length of the trip. Cold camps reduce pack weight and cleanup efforts. In the winter, the ability to eat hot meals and consume hot beverages is a must to maintain and restore a normal body temperature to avoid hypothermia.

Suggested Food List

[R] = Repackage food and other items before a hike to eliminate initial trash.

Cold Camp (No stove)

◈ Energy bars; electrolyte drink mix (**breakfast**).
◈ Peanut butter and date sandwich on whole grain round flat bread (**lunch**). Make in advance.
◈ Tuna [in foil pouch] in tortilla wrap (**dinner**).
◈ Jerky, salami, tuna, or other meats in foil pouch.
◈ Crackers [R]; sesame sticks [R].
◈ Cheese (small "wheel") in wax packaging such as Gouda or Edam.
◈ Almond & cashew mix (custom trail mix) [R].

❖ Chocolate (Peanut M&M's) [R].
❖ Fig Newtons [R].
❖ Dried fruit mix: dates, raisins, plums, apples, mango, apricots, pineapple [R].
❖ Hard candy: Tic Tac [R], Jolly Rancher [R], Nestlé Nips coffee [R].

Hot Meals

(Add lightweight stove system) The first 5 items need hot water only—no cooking reduces flame time, which conserves fuel so less fuel will need to be packed. Cooking in an instant also requires smaller cleanups, conserving nonrenewable middle-of-the-trail water in Grand Canyon's backcountry. The last two items require short cook times.

❖ Oatmeal [instant] packets; instant coffee; instant tea.
❖ Cup of Noodles [R]; add slices of meat.
❖ Dehydrated beans & season mix.
❖ Instant stuffing mix; add slices of meat.
❖ Instant potatoes [R]; add slices of meat.
❖ Lipton-Knorr's "Sides" seasoned pasta-rice blends [R]; add slices of meat.
❖ Macaroni & cheese [R]; add slices of meat.

Ancient kitchenware. Ancestral Puebloan pottery. (GRCA 3130)

Pay It Forward

Overnight stays in Grand Canyon National Park require a Backcountry Use Permit. Hikers are expected to practice minimum impact travel, which will preserve the canyon system for future generations. We are entrusted with a stewardship today that will leave a legacy "not only for tomorrow but for the day after tomorrow."

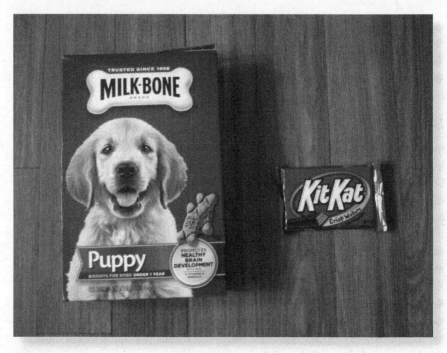

Emergency food for extreme backcountry hiking delays. One extra day of food for rationing—some extra healthy snack foods. Then what? Which one would you eat first? You are right, the Kit Kat®. The Kit Kat®, however, would be eaten too soon. That's why it is absolutely essential to bring an emergency food that will not be quickly consumed. I bring nine dog biscuits. Potentially: 1 for breakfast, 1 for lunch, 1 for dinner to spread over three days. Dog biscuits are slow to eat as they are extremely hard. However, they are nonperishable and nutritious. One will have to be in a tricky situation to force feed on dog biscuits making them go the distance. What will your emergency food be?

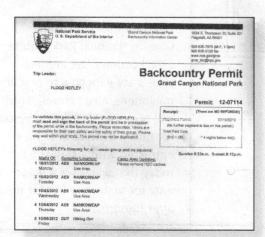

Search guideline. The Backcountry Use Permit itinerary becomes a tool used by the National Park Service should a hiker become overdue.

GRAND CANYON MINIMUM IMPACT "LEAVE NO TRACE" TRAVEL

Obtain current regulations as new management practices may have gone into effect.

Forest Service Development Road Use

◈ Obtain current travel information before departing onto a network of Forest Development and National Park Service Roads as use restrictions change.

◈ Avoid driving over sapling trees, brush, and grasses by remaining on established roads. Respect and do not approach wildlife.

◈ Do not cut or disturb vegetation.

◈ Drive around streambeds, hillsides, and meadows. Do not establish new wheel tracks and roads.

◈ Carry out (pack out) all trash.

◈ Whenever possible, choose a previously used campsite to reduce environmental impact.

◈ Camp away from streambeds and with sufficient separation from other campers.

◈ Choose a camp stove over an open fire. Fire restrictions may be in effect making it not possible for open fires and, in extreme cases, no charcoal briquette fires.

◈ Choose a toilet site at least 200 feet away from water, camp, and streambed sites. Dig a 6-inch deep hole and make deposit. When done, refill hole immediately.

◈ Camp at least a quarter-mile from water sources to allow animal access.

◈ Sometimes roads will be closed due to wildlife habitat protection, erosion control, temporary use restrictions, seasonal closures, and fire danger.

Inner Canyon Hiking

◈ Stay together. The *hike leader* should "take up the rear" (last in the line of hikers) in and out of the canyon. This safety method provides the ability for the hike leader to *shepherd* the group. Some exceptions to taking up the rear include when a trail is questionable, dangerous, or hard to find.

◈ Stay on designated trails. Do not shortcut switchbacks. Shortcutting accelerates erosion, causes dangerous rock falls, and takes more time and energy than remaining on a route. When exploring off-trail, choose dry creeks and slick rock as travel paths. Biotic soils are easily damaged and take decades to recover.

◈ Respect the wildlife. Do not approach or feed.

◈ The process of human waste: select an area that is at least 200 feet from water sources, trails, and campsites. Dig a hole 6 inches deep, disturbing the soil as little as possible; deposit feces; pack out used toilet paper in plastic bags with other trash. Do not burn trash, as wildfires have started by burning trash and toilet paper. Overland, do not urinate into streams. However, when near the Colorado River, it has been determined that urinating directly into the river's current is the best overall environmental remedy.

◈ It is unlawful to disturb archeological sites. The Grand Canyon human history is fragmented. Undisturbed sites will provide clues to archaeologists that might one day complete the story.

◈ Spelunking (exploring caves or mines) requires an additional permit endorsement, beyond the Backcountry Use Permit, issued by the National Park Service.

Inner Canyon Camping

◈ Select a campsite, when possible, that has been previously used or locate a site on slick rock out of dry creeks and washes to avoid flash floods. "At large" means one may occupy any undeveloped hard ground locale within a Use Area. Washes look ideal as campsites, however camping in a stream bed is hazardous as they are prone to flash flooding.

◈ Protect Inner Canyon water sources by not washing clothes, dishes, and body in them. Contain water and take it 200 feet away from the source. Discard dirty water over a vegetated area.

◈ Store food in a steal mesh bag or cookie tin to keep animals out.

Slick rock camp. My camp on top of dusty slick rock is one form of minimum impact travel. This site, like several others, is located in the Kaibab National Forest opposite the Grand Canyon National Park Boundary Line fence.

❖ "Pack it in pack it out" Inner Canyon cargo policy. Food scraps— "micro trash"—must be picked up and packed out with primary trash accumulation.

Trash collection. In Bright Angel Campground at the bottom of the canyon, trash was accumulated in a ziplock bag. At the end of the stay at that campsite, I stuff paper trash into a tiny empty meat can and then compact it with a cobblestone to reduce the overall bulk. Notice through the process of outer package elimination, before the trip started, there isn't much total trash.

❖ A valid fishing license is required for all fishing.

GRAND CANYON EQUIPMENT CHECKLIST: ESSENTIAL MINIMUMS

The following is a suggested equipment list and is meant as a guideline. Individual needs may vary to the point of adjusting a selection. Consult the National Park Service for conditions that may require additional items based on the most current trail and weather conditions. (See Personal Safety)

Scrutinize all gear to keep the pack light. As a general rule of thumb, a pack should weigh approximately no more than one-fourth of a person's body weight. In any season, bring all gear to the rim for final assessment, such as weather changes, that may be necessary to complete a hike safely.

Based on conscientious gear selection, including food and two gallons of water, my backpack weighs 43 pounds for a five-day, non-winter, trek. By keeping the backpack as trim as possible, room and additional pack weight remain to take on extra gear to handle inclement weather.

All-Season Gear

◈ **Backpack:** Consider **internal frame:** low center of gravity, requires strategy loading, and retains body moisture. **External frame:** high center of gravity, easier to load, and body moisture evaporates as there is a gap between pack and body.

My backpack of choice is the internal frame. While it takes a little practice to load (use individual color-coded stuff sacks to identify contents, i.e.: clothes, yellow sack; food, blue sack, etc.), in the long run the internal frame backpack is more efficient making a tough scramble easier due to the lower center of gravity and the retention/conservation of water through perspiration (both warm and cold weather). In the winter, because an internal frame pack "hugs" the body, it helps to retain body warmth. For all reasons, this is why expeditions use the internal frame—good for Mt. Everest, even better for the Grand Canyon.

Solo hikers need to be self-sufficient requiring a greater amount of weight in non-shared gear: "You carry the tent and I'll carry the cook gear." As a side note, do not separate the tent from the tent poles or the stove and utensils from the fuel cell to divide the weight. Both gear items become useless should the party become separated.

❖ **Boots:** Consider good insoles and crisscrossing tread, with a snug fit where heal is comfortably nestled back into the footwear creating and preserving toe room.

❖ **Water containment (see also *bulk water carrier*): Minimum capacity, at least one gallon per person per day.** Wide-mouth Nalgene® brand bottles are the most reliable means to carry and purify water. The bottle tolerates both freezing (winter) without cracking and non-direct flame boiling temperatures without melting or losing shape (alternate water purification method) with reusability. Water consumption needs go up with the temperature. Water is a Grand Canyon hiker's most valuable item and should be considered their most precious commodity.

In Grand Canyon hiking, those with containment devices totaling less than one gallon [per person] are considered "toys." The Grand Canyon can create its own weather patterns outside the range of prediction. At times the weather forecast cannot account for a sudden shift in the Grand Canyon weather pattern when a "cool" 100-degree late spring or early fall day went up to 110 degrees or more. **Empty bottle space** can be used to store extra food or clothing items.

The Equipment List

To be used all-inclusive by the trip leader (person named on the Backcountry Use Permit). Some items will be group redundant such as a stove that can be shared. Some items, such as moleskin, will need to be plentiful to aid the entire group. With knowledge of use, the items listed are Grand Canyon performance proven and are just as useful on the Main Corridor trails as they are in the backcountry. My backpack is cookie cutter loaded. It is practically the same whether I'm hiking the Main Corridor, such as the Bright Angel or Kaibab Trails, or as on this one, the Nankoweap Trail. While on group hikes, I use the Main Corridor to test and prove my gear selection. One example is the ability to treat water in the Main Corridor. Even though there is potable water on tap, it is often that the waterline breaks, interrupting trans-canyon domestic water service.

◈ While *hydration bladders* are convenient, they are delicate and prone to leaking due to punctures and imperfections at the connection to the bladder and also at the bite valve. Many hikers have also *out-drank* their hike as the water is deliciously close to the mouth at the bite valve. It is equally important to remain consistently hydrated with the ability to *float* to the next renewable water source for complete rehydration.

Water is bodily lost through sweat, urine, feces, and breathing. Under NORMAL and IDEAL circumstances, someone in reasonable physical condition can live an estimated 3–5 days without water. In the Grand Canyon and vicinity, someone who is physically overexerted in the heat without replacing fluids and electrolytes can in fact die in a matter of several hours. (See *First Aid Kit: Life Threatening Conditions*)

> **Manifest:** Bring gear to the rim that may be needed in the event of a change in the weather. It's better to have the selection than to be without.

◈ **Bulk water carrier: Minimum capacity, one gallon per person.** Four one-quart bottles or collapsible tote to cache along the trail. This brings the total water containment per person to TWO gallons. It is important to have the ability to increase water portability especially on those summer days when temperatures increase or there is a delay en route.

◈ **Footwear traction device:** crampons or other devices for an icy or muddy route should it rain or snow depending on seasonal travel. **CAUTION:** The Nankoweap Trail follows an elevated and exposed narrow ledge-way for miles. Use good judgment in all climatic conditions before traveling any portion of the route.

◈ **Crew socks:** wicking and padded for impact.

◈ **Trekking poles:** Trekking poles require minimal practice. Once the skill is acquired, trekking poles are an asset as the hiker can walk with increased efficiency.

◈ **Wide brim hat:** UPF rated—portable shade.

◈ **Windbreaker/rain jacket combo.**

◈ **Flannel or hybrid material long sleeve shirt:** insulation.

◈ **Compression briefs:** moisture wicking; eliminates skin-to-skin contact.

◈ **T-shirt & long sleeve shirt:** UPF rated; cool and warm keeping; moisture wicking.

◈ **Pants long/short combo:** UPF rated; moisture wicking.

◈ **Ground sheets (2):** "space blanket" style that is shiny on one side (reflects the sun and heat) and the other side that is opaque (usually red or blue or green) to use as a body wrap to retain body heat; one rain-fly (lightweight waterproof tarp with grommets all around the edges).

Micro Gear (All Seasons)

◈ **Map & Compass:** To reduce bulk and weight, make a copy of the section you're going to hike and include a sufficient surrounding area illustrating other possible alternate routes.

◈ **Flashlight:** A head lamp is ideal for use with trekking poles; include several extra lighting devices. NOTE: In a group hike, it is prudent for everyone in the group to carry the same lighting make and model. A spare device provides the opportunity to make quick repairs by swapping out parts.

Grand Canyon specific. The author's micro-gear/med bag setup for Inner Canyon solo hiking, yet group effective, since 1980. The bag is always loaded into the backpack last so it can be accessed first. On solo hikes, you are your own worst enemy, therefore, you have to be your own buddy system.

◈ **Pocketknife combo:** Small single blade/scissors/tweezers.

◈ **Multi-tool:** Small as possible to include pliers.

◈ **Lighter & Matches:** two forms of fire making as a failsafe redundant system; matches should be the water-windproof type and, as an additional failsafe, should be stored in at least two separate areas of the backpack. Both items should be stored in a watertight container.

◈ **Whistle:** low energy output, minimal effort alert device. Some packs have a whistle molded into the sternum strap buckle or you can lanyard a whistle to the backpack within reach.

◈ **Sewing needle & thread.**

◈ **Duct tape:** short supply rolled onto an ink pen casing shortened to the same width as the tape. Duct tape is ideal for footwear repair including re-mating a lug sole to the upper sole. **Unique use of duct tape:** I have repaired a punctured water bottle by

While a wide variety of gear is nice to have and may look desirable at the retail outlet, a hiker has to be able to lift it out in the field.

inserting a plug of Chapstick® into the hole and then covering the plug with a strip of tape.

◈ **Utility cord:** Paracord (parachute cord) is multi-tasking and eliminates a multitude of micro gear. Paracord is multipurpose by length (100 feet), and test (550 lbs), and shoelace size by gauge (5/32-inch). Paracord can be used to replace a boot lace, guy a rain-fly, hoist a pack down or up a vertical section of route, or in extreme measures aid in a rescue. Military specifications schedule 7 inner cords within a "sheath," or wrap. Each of the 7 inner cords is made of 3 individual strands, which can be unraveled as thread to sew a repair.

◈ **Survival handsaw:** a wire band with aggressive teeth and a finger "hand-hold" ring at each end. Fundamental alpine zone forest tool where temperatures are much lower and where cutting dead and downed wood for shelter and for firewood might be permitted.

On the way out. Reconfiguring equipment in the backpack to make the adjustment for return water cache on Tilted Mesa. Notice the rock "paperweight" on the foreground plastic bag.

Wet and Cold Weather Gear
(In Addition to All-Season Gear)

◈ **Tent:** including dedicated tent ground sheet.

◈ **Foam sleeping pad:** provides insulation from the cold ground.

◈ **Sleeping bag:** synthetic fill; light and compact with appropriate degree rating.

◈ **Boots:** four season.

◈ **Warm clothes—wool or synthetic:** socks, pants, upper body, knit cap, long johns, parka, mittens/gloves. (Note: with the sacrifice being in the loss of dexterity, mittens keep the hands warmer as fingers remain united.)

◈ **Mountain stove and fuel:** I am currently using the MSR® Pocket Rocket® with a hybrid propane-butane fuel.

◈ **Cook set:** pot with lid; porcelain-covered metal cup (metal can take direct heat from the stove and the porcelain coating allows the mouth to make contact with the cup without sticking to the lips); metal cooking/eating utensils combo; metal pot clamp and or padded pot grip; biodegradable soap. (Note: biodegradable soap may not make contact with Inner Canyon water sources such as streams and creeks.)

Grand Canyon First-Aid Kit

The following is a suggested first-aid kit list and is intended as a guideline. First-aid kit contents will vary based on individual needs and determined by personal health history in consultation with your personal physician. Consult the National Park Service for the most current trail and weather conditions that may require additional items. (See Personal Safety)

Prescription and non-prescription "over the counter" items such as relief from allergy, tooth ache, stomach ache, pain reliever, water purification method, moleskin, ankle wrap, antibacterial ointment, bandaids, gauze, cotton swabs, medical tape, "chemical" cold pack, sunscreen, lip balm, and insect repellant. Also include signal mirror, nail clippers, toilet paper & trowel, note paper, and small pencil (ink freezes in winter).

Recognizing Life-Threatening Emergencies

CAUTION: *You are responsible for your own and your group's safety.* Recognize the symptoms and avoid these life threatening conditions by resting often, eating smart, keeping cool and shaded or warm and dry as defined by the season. (See Equipment Check List: water containment) The following is a helpful guideline:

◈ DEHYDRATION AND HEAT EXHAUSTION: Symptoms include dry mouth, thirst, headache, dry skin that lacks elasticity, sleepiness, lack of sweating, decreased urine yield, muscle cramps, nausea, and dizziness/light-headedness.

Treatment: Help move person into shaded area or make shade with a space blanket (hold or suspend blanket with trekking poles in such a way that promotes side venting). Replace fluids with water and electrolytes.

◈ HEAT STROKE (over heating to death) can follow dehydration and heat exhaustion. Symptoms include high body temperature of 104 degrees and higher, racing heart rate, rapid breathing, throbbing headache, confusion, unconsciousness.

Treatment: Reduce core body temperature by placing person in a shaded area or make shade with a space blanket (do not wrap person; hold or suspend blanket with trekking poles in such a way that promotes side venting). Remove excess clothing for ventilation. Wet the removed clothing and use as towels and place on head, neck, armpits, and groin. Mist (without depleting drinking water) and fan person. Gradually replace body fluids with water and electrolyte drinks.

◈ HYPOTHERMIA (freezing to death): Symptoms include shivering and chattering (clicking) teeth, slurred speech or mumbling, stumbling, confusion, drowsiness and low energy, apathy, weak pulse, shallow breathing, body temperature at or below 95 degrees, poor decision making.

Treatment: Warm the body back to a normal temperature by gently moving person out of cold and wind to a warm, dry place. If unable to move then create shelter with tent and space blankets. Remove wet clothing (cut away clothing if necessary to avoid jarring the person), cover the person with blankets, dry clothing; cover head leaving face exposed. Insulate the person's body from the cold ground. Share body heat by making skin-to-skin contact. Then cover both bodies with blankets. Provide warm beverages when person is alert and able to swallow.

◈ HYPONATREMIA (water intoxication): is the dilution of sodium from the body. The body is already depleted, therefore, hyponatremia can set in. When this occurs, water levels rise and cells begin to swell and can cause severe health issues including coma and death. Symptoms include nausea, vomiting, headache, fatigue, muscle weakness and cramps, seizures, and coma.

Treatment: Avoid this condition, plan ahead and stay on a hydration/food schedule that equalizes the body. (See Provisions)

Blister Treatment: Pre-blister and Post-blister

After the possible complications of exhaustion and the logistics of the lack of water, one of the most common ailments encountered when hiking the Grand Canyon is blisters. The following is a helpful guideline.

Pre-blister Treatment

Treat the known prone blister area, or "hot-spot" (the abrasion point on the foot before blister forms):
1. Place gauze over known area or "hot spot."
2. Cover gauze generously with bandages.
3. Cover this dressing with an over-lapping swatch of moleskin so as to adhere to a broad margin of healthy skin.
4. Cuff and roll sock onto foot so as not to peel fresh moleskin.
5. Put on footwear.

Post-blister Treatment

1. Cleanse affected area with clean water to remove body fluids and abrasive debris such as dirt particles. Follow up with an antibacterial ointment such as Neosporin®.
2. Place and hold thick non-stick style pure gauze swatch over blister.
3. Frame gauze with bandages. Cover gauze with bandages.
4. Place large swatch of overlapping moleskin over gauze and bandage dressing to make sufficient contact onto unaffected skin to keep entire dressing adhered and in place.
5. Cuff and roll sock over dressing.
6. With extremely loose laces and the footwear pulled wide open, gently slip footwear on over sock.
7. Allow for foot to adjust to refined conditions. Foot "body heat" will cause moleskin to configure to foot.

> Moleskin provides the true barrier between an abrasive point and the skin. Bandage strips are typically insufficient. Moleskin will peel "with a tug" from healthy skin, sometimes leaving an easily removed gummy residue.
>
> **Warning:** Do not place moleskin directly on a blister. Moleskin is a secondary skin and will adhere to human skin and will cause further harm to the affected area(s) and will have to be surgically removed.

8. After hike, remove moleskin and dressing treatment, in reverse order by gently removing footwear and socks and gently peeling off moleskin and dressing treatment, being careful not to tug affected skin area.
9. Cleanse and treat and bandage area and wear clean, white (no ink dyes), 100% cotton socks and non-heeled sandals.
10. Seek medical attention for follow-up procedure and further treatment.

Foot warmer. It is not uncommon for a scorpion during its nightly investigation for insect prey to enter cozy footwear. Because *Centruroides sculpturatus* climb trees and live under tree bark, hence the common name "bark scorpion," hanging boots from foliage branches does not inhibit a scorpion from entering. It should be included in the routine of all Grand Canyon Inner Canyon hikers to shake out footwear and gear before wearing. The photo was taken at the bottom of the canyon in the stone corral at Phantom Ranch under black light.

EPILOGUE: AN INDIAN SUMMER

Fred Anderson—Andy—and I still walk the canyon rim and recall our time together with our small core group, and the few times together when we went through thick and thicker. We've dealt with the heat of an Inner Canyon day and running short of water on the Tonto Trail. We've handled a lack of shade and contorted our bodies into the shade-shape of a scraggly cat claw tree casting its contorted shadow onto a rounded Tapeats Sandstone boulder, to simply combating insects in Bright Angel Campground. Each and every time, Andy taught me to understand the accomplishment of the succession of the single footstep.

In my early solo years with the canyon, I ran severely short of water—call it running out of water. I was on the Tonto Trail heading west between the bottom of the Hance Trail and the Grand View Trail. I underestimated my water needs and ran short as the canyon's temperatures elevated above the summer forecast. I describe what happened by remembering those old cowboy movies when the stranded cowboy runs out of water.

> "Maybe you're dialed into the canyon," my brother Rye once said of me. "You can take the man out of the canyon, but you can't take the canyon out of the man."

When he finally comes to water over hot desert miles, he falls down face first and drinks desperately—that's how it happens. When I at last reached Hance Creek, I fell down face first into the wispy stream and drank with gusto, feeling I had no time left to purify water.

Now at age fifty, with years and with miles of Grand Canyon experience, my solo hike of the Nankoweap Trail began on Saddle Mountain at the end of Forest Development Road 610 where I parked my pickup truck and chocked the wheels with cobbles of Kaibab Limestone. It is here on top of Saddle Mountain contiguously north of Point Imperial where Trail #57 begins and the forest of ponderosa pine and aspen yield to the Grand Canyon. It was the first week of October, 2012.

I sleep cold so as not to be too cozy to wake up and be on the move when first light rolls around. My pack was loaded per my manifest. On the tailgate of my pickup truck, I made the final assessment of the gear I intended to bring down into the canyon, but just as significant, the security of the gear I intended to leave behind to keep my backpack trim without compromising safety. I tracked the weather for one week prior to the start of my hike and confirmed the extended forecast with the North Kaibab Ranger District. Under an almost full moon, there was no rain on the way and the days were to be warm and the nights chilly and breezy.

My hiking strategy included rationing water and backpacking the first three miles, which is Trail #57, to the Grand Canyon National Park Boundary Line fence and camp in the Kaibab National Forest just on the other side of the boundary line from the park. The next day would be the official start date of my hike. On that next day, I hiked the eight miles from the Grand Canyon National Park trailhead to the junction with Nankoweap Creek and on to the Colorado River.

On the way into the canyon, the end of the trail is where the canyon says the end of the trail is. The canyon usually decides the end of the trail by the provision of a flowing creek or river water—something a hiker cannot do without. Sometimes it's an area dripping with shade, another midday value. But always there must be water, either from a natural source or from a rationed water bottle. There seems to be nothing more adventuresome in the Grand Canyon than not knowing exactly where a trail ends. A map reveals only so much. The recesses of the Inner Canyon conceal a next leg and side canyons swing in deeply out of foresight. Eventually the footstep carries the hiker to the short-term goal. This time it was Marion Point and the cozy campsites nestled in the juniper trees. I wasn't at Marion to stay, but it was an intermediate objective. Around the hairpin in the route, the cliffside seasonal spring was not flowing.

I carry a swatch of aluminum foil in my pack for the purpose of pressing and molding it to a cliff face below a seep so I can collect ten drops of water at a time and have them funnel into a wide-mouth water bottle. I came up with this piece of "equipment" after the hike along the Tonto Trail below the South Rim where I ran out of water. While climbing up the east side of Horseshoe Mesa, Page Spring (also called Miner's Spring) is met adjacent to Peter Berry's Last Chance Mine. At the spring, the water is in the form of droplets—and where wasps are numerous. Before carrying the foil, I sat or crouched under a seep and collected water drop by drop. As the wasps buzzed and lighted on my ear lobes, I concluded that they were virtually harmless and there for the same reason I was. Collecting the cool spring water was essential for survival and the wasps are essential to the canyon ecosystem.

Beyond Marion Point, Tilted Mesa became a near reality and by the time I landed on its creamy slick rock cap, the comfort of walking the ledge-ways between the point and mesa ended and the trail soon began what the National Park

Service describes as VERY STEEP. I removed my pack on top of the mesa and put the water bottles and food of my cache in a stuff sack—the same red stuff sack I've been using since the early '80s to keep my cache clean. When I left the reserve, I was already looking forward to its freshness upon my return. Because it was still early, I didn't stay on the mesa and soon departed for Nankoweap Creek and the Colorado River.

Apart from the mileage between the trailheads and the mesa top, and the mesa's base and Nankoweap Creek, there is a journey within the journey that is found within the mileage on the steep rocky debris that makes up Tilted Mesa's steep sidewall features. As ranger John Riffey would describe a trail section like this one, which can be found on the Lava Route in the Toroweap district of Grand Canyon that he once patrolled, the slope "rests at the steepest angle of repose." I jostled my way down the slopes and made it to the sandy bottom of a wash, then turned easterly and contoured Tilted Mesa's midsection as shale clanked together under my boots. When I

Navajo Indian Reservation

Tilted Mesa

Marion Point

Transitions, ramps, and descents. No switchbacks. Not visible to the naked eye from Point Imperial, the route down Tilted Mesa is in a series of talus, rock, and cobblestone slaloms.

stepped off the last of the mesa and onto the Tapeats Sandstone slope, I was also almost to the creek when it got hot, about 95 degrees—cool by Inner Canyon standards. It was high noon on this shadeless trail. In the first week of October, summer is still making its exit.

I descended onto the bank of Nankoweap Creek and drank the last of my water that I brought from home. At the creek—first things first—I drew water from the creek and purified a gallon of drinking water. I unpacked my bedroll and spread it out under the cool branches of the cottonwood tree that marks the trail and creek transition and stayed the night, the river still three miles away. It cooled off as the dark night settled in before moonrise. I put on a flannel shirt and fell asleep on top of my ground sheet. When I woke up chilly later that night, I added a windbreaker for insulation and rolled up again in my ground sheet and fell right back to sleep. When I awoke in the morning, I was glad to be here and at the same time already devising my exit plan. And I wasn't even at the river yet. As I said before, "I'll be my own worst enemy and my own buddy system and wing man." Planning the steps ahead was essential to a successful hike on a trail not *like* this one—but *this one*—the Nankoweap Trail.

Standing on the creek bed, and aiming downstream at the Colorado River, the first step to determining the path of least resistance without a route-path is to make a first step. There never really is a best way to know until you are walking. Just what side of a backcountry creek will make for the best path over a cobblestone strewn side canyon floor has to be encountered and, most likely,

First sight. The Nankoweap Ruin from near river level.

adjustments will have to be made. And the way back from the river may be a little different than the way chosen to the river. Following the path of least resistance, down and then up a streambed, just works out that way. The deer tracks that I saw on the way in I did not see on the way back.

At the Colorado River, Nankoweap Rapid flowed vigorously between the Marble Canyon wall below the Blue Moon Bench formation and the broad beaches of the Nankoweap Creek Delta. Above the beaches on the Nankoweap Mesa is what may be called the centerpiece of the region—the Nankoweap Ruin. The granary is approximately 500 feet above the river and was used to store seeds and grain and other food items essential to the survival of the Ancestral Puebloan. Once called Anasazi, these people resided on the cooler rims in the summer, such as the Walhalla Glades, and the warmer Inner Canyon in the winter. As I sat on the ledge at the granary, I wondered what it was like for the people who lived here day to day and season to season. I could imagine the adults engaged in conversations of wisdom regarding the duration of winter and deciding when they had enough food stored. While the adults planned, their children must have been laughing and running and playing on the riverbank.

Storage in the sky. The Nankoweap granary was placed high above the river to protect its contents from a raging high river. Centuries ago, long before any man-made dam blocked the historic Colorado River system, the Grand Canyon saw virtually the last, and took the brunt, of all flooding upper river systems such as the Green, the Dolores, and the San Juan. Prehistoric driftwood found lodged high in the canyon walls attest to the reasoning behind such a safe storage practice.

Pantry. Nankoweap granary ruin.

A look inside.

Approaching the end of my permitted moment of reflection in the canyon, I allowed time for a two-day exit out of the canyon. I moved my camp from the Colorado River upstream on the Nankoweap Creek to the junction with the stream and the descending trail as a prelude to the scramble up Tilted Mesa. I decided that I would sleep cold without my flannel shirt until I woke with teeth chattering from the chill in the air and then pick up and go under the moonlight. Before bed, I purified a gallon of water dedicated for my steep hike to the top of the mesa, where my cache awaited me on the mesa capstone. At 11:30 p.m. under the full moon, with my gear already loaded before dark, I picked up my bedroll and fastened it to my backpack. At midnight I swiftly departed Nankoweap Creek. I couldn't forget my pillow because I use the toe end of my boots covered with my hat and I was already wearing them. The logistics of a lighter pack come from making double use of gear items or simply making do without non-critical gear.

Grand Canyon trails and routes glow a bit under moonlight. The disturbed earth of the trails, even when they're narrow or topical, seem like smoldering embers where the moonlight casts tracing shadows down the length of the cobbles and the rocks and the pebbles embedded in the pathway. I've walked the canyon trails many times by night—sometimes out of necessity to escape the heat of an Inner Canyon day. The knack of walking the canyon trails by night is acquired on the National Park Service maintained routes, such as the Bright Angel and the Kaibab Trails. It's a learning process that may need to be employed in the canyon at one time or another. Walking the canyon by night may seem in foresight beyond one's ability, but it will just come naturally as the occasion arises. I'm convinced that if I can get ahead of the heat of the Inner Canyon day, even just a little bit before the possibility of losing the trail, it will be an asset to the ultimate short-term, next-destination goal. Call it a head start.

Here on the Nankoweap Trail, I initiated my exit in the middle of the night. I climbed the steep slope out of the creek bed and made my way across the gentle grade of Tapeats Sandstone. Walking between abrupt black Kaibab scrub brush and toe-height prickly pear cactus under the moonlight, the route was very faint but, to me, comprehensible. I negotiated the wash below the crumbling Bright Angel Shale blocks of Tilted Mesa's southerly apron. Here is where I questioned myself as to the correct way to go. I didn't remember walking in this direction on the way in. But it was the trail. When I came to the cairn I had set on the way in, and in the beam of my headlamp saw ahead to another recognizable cairn set, a feeling of great comfort came over me and I declared, "Blessings to all cairn builders."

Then the going got rough, as anticipated, on the ascent of Titled Mesa's midsection. I stopped frequently not only to rest and drink, but to also increase the realization that in just a matter of hours—long hours—I will have to relinquish this awesome trek to the passing of time. By the hike's design under a full moon and moonlight, I casually reached Tilted Mesa about an hour before sunrise, taking ample time to enjoy the Inner Canyon by moonlight. The canyon takes on a dissimilar countenance to itself under moonlight. The buttes and points and terraces compose tethered distant shadows down into the canyon. Mt. Hayden becomes frosted in moonlight. And down below, the topsoil of the Nankoweap Basin is radiant, coming forth as otherworldly.

On Tilted Mesa, I watched the day break over the Navajo Indian Reservation's broad tableland of Blue Moon Bench. On top of the lofty block surface of Tilted Mesa during that sunrise, I was reminded of the Bible verse in the book of Isaiah: *Heaven is My throne and the earth is My footstool. Where is the house that you will build Me? And where is the place of My rest?* Meaning the Lord cannot be contained and that there is no need for a physical structure. I was also reminded of astronaut, Neil Armstrong, and what he said of the moon's surface. That it reminded him of the deserts of the Southwest. I can see where he would feel that way, as I can see how the moonlit Inner Canyon might bear a resemblance to the lunar surface.

Moonset. Early morning in Nankoweap Creek on the route to the Colorado River.

Increasingly, hiking the canyon by moonlight reminds me of my astronaut hero, Michael Collins. Neil Armstrong made the historic first step on the moon, with Buzz Aldrin stepping next. However, I've always been fascinated by the heroics of astronaut Michael Collins who had the duty, and will, to stay behind and pilot the orbiting command module, *Columbia*. On the dark side of the moon, Collins said, "Outside my window, I can see stars—and that is all. Where I know the moon to be, there is simply a black void, the moon's presence is defined solely by the absence of stars." From the bottom of the Inner Canyon, when there is no moon, the pitch black Inner Gorge's presence is also defined solely by the absence of stars under a star-loaded northern Arizona night sky.

Collins made the flight of the *Eagle* lander to the lunar surface and the walk on the moon possible for Neil and Buzz. Sometimes called the "forgotten astronaut," many don't immediately recall Michael Collins. In 1982, I had made another exit from the Inner Canyon on the South Rim's Hermit Trail, where there was a family silently peering into the canyon. Nearby, I removed my dusty backpack and set it in the bed of my pickup.

"Hi, how are you?" I said.

"Fine. How are you?" the father said. "Did you come up from the bottom?"

"I'm wonderful, thanks. Yes, I left the bottom this morning," I said.

Looking at his watch, he said, "But it's only eight o'clock in the morning."

"Yeah, days start early in the summer at Grand Canyon. I hike the cooler parts of the day and sometimes at night," I said.

"You hike at night?" he said.

"It just comes natural … the canyon is amazing under moonlight," I said.

Sometimes I feel like an astronaut—hiking the canyon by night—with a view similar to what Michael Collins might have had for a day in 1969. Like an astronauts' "right stuff," solo hikers of the Grand Canyon acquire their own right stuff before such an uncertain undertaking. Those that intend to hike solo should first have traveled in groups, for a time. A buddy-system safety minimum in hiking is a group of four. Should someone become ill or injured, one can stay with that person, and two can go for help. A hiker of the Grand Canyon is on Grand Canyon terms—learning the canyon's way of doing things.

From the sublimity of Tilted Mesa I was only obligated to hike back to the Boundary Line fence where I had made my first camp. After sunrise from the mesa, though, I felt I could reach the forest service trailhead and my pickup truck. After traveling the ledge-ways to Marion Point, where the seep was not active, and onward to the small set of switchbacks in the Supai Sandstone, I rested for a long while and had lunch at the same spot where I had camped the first night of the hike. I reenergized and picked myself up and continued on through the undulating hills of Saddle Mountain, where in this time alone in the Grand Canyon backcountry, this hilly section brought me back to the 1970s and a lesson in Grand Canyon canyoneering.

This '70s hike was partly on the River Trail and I was hiking toward the Bright Angel Trail in the wee hours of the night with Andy (who devised starting hikes out at 2:00 a.m. in the summer) and his nephew Charlie and our core group. Charlie grew tired of the River Trail, which dips and rises along the Colorado. We were hiking up and out of the canyon and, to the six-foot-two Charlie, going downhill after climbing uphill was unacceptable. For which he would look back, and through the dark of night ask his uncle, "Uncle Fred? This trail goes down again?" And Andy would reply in a calm long, "Yeeess." Charlie, who was at the front of the hike would exclaim, "We're supposed to be going out!" He continued walking and came up on another rise in the trail and stopped on the edge of a broad terrace a couple hundred feet above the river. This time he didn't ask his uncle about the trail character, but yelled it out, *"This trail goes down again!?"*

I suppose it wouldn't have mattered too much, but it just so happened that in the middle of the night, Charlie had stopped just short of stepping on—but standing directly over—two sleeping bags and two exhausted people too tired to continue on. The pair had put down for the night right on the trail's edge and were startled awake and now distressed facing a very big and irritated man. Charlie apologized and was quiet the rest of the way. A funny story indeed, but it was a good fundamental learning lesson. The couple that almost got pulverized into the gravel of the River Trail by the six-foot plus Navy man had nothing to do with the lesson that I learned that night.

The lesson learned is that the canyon trails will sometimes elude a hiker as they dip and rise and swing into the bays of side canyons. But no matter. The real lesson here is that if a trail is fourteen miles long it doesn't matter if it goes up or down or sideways—miles are miles and each forward step has value. The slight exception to this lesson is the Nankoweap Trail. While each forward step still has value, it is a long way on the ledge-ways before Tilted Mesa, and the objective is to get to the bottom of the canyon but you can't keep walking laterally. That means when the trail finally descends, it will descend sharply, rapidly, and steeply. And that's what the Nankoweap Trail does below the capstone of Tilted Mesa.

In 1963, within the designated park boundaries of his day, forty-one-year-old Colin Fletcher made his classic, air-drop supported, Grand Canyon National Park length-long Inner Canyon solo walk. He entered the canyon from the southwest at Hualapai Hilltop—the trail to Havasupai (Supai). In *The Man Who Walked Through Time*, Fletcher makes his exit from the Inner Canyon on the Nankoweap Trail on the sprawling edge of Saddle Mountain, the former inclusive eastern park boundary, and hikes his way along the fire road (now called the Point Imperial Trail) to Point Imperial. This is inferred as he walked two hours to a paved road. The only other paved road in the area would have been Arizona State Route 67, which is fourteen miles away. Fletcher was also tired—walking the two miles in two hours. At the close of his trek, Fletcher conveys nothing much different than what others, including myself, echo at the end of a long hike:

I climbed up onto the North Rim ... Sunlight flashed on a row of automobiles ... I stepped out of the trees onto pavement and walked toward the cars ... People were moving among them ... A man ran his eye over my battered backpack and smiled and said: "Having yourself a good time?" "Yes, thanks," I said, and smiled back. My journey was over. I rejoined the present.

Back on Saddle Mountain, I find my pickup truck waiting for me, the wheels still chocked with the Kaibab Limestone rocks where I wedged them. Andy instructed me to chock my vehicle's wheels when I leave it for a hike—these days I continue to do so more for traditional reasons than as a safety precaution. Between Nankoweap Creek and the time I reached my pickup truck, I enjoyed all my ample water supply—two gallons—twice as much water than I drank on the hike in.

I lowered the tailgate of my pickup and dismounted from my backpack for the last time this trip and switched out my boots for loose-laced running shoes. On the tailgate, I heated a can of chili over the backpacking stove and small cook set that I chose not to take into the canyon based on the extended weather report. Chili with saltine crackers and water with a berry-flavored electrolyte mix—scrumptious. I ate in the canyon—meaning a large protein bar at the beginning of the day (sunrise) and at the end of the day (usually last light) tuna wrapped in a wheat tortilla. In between sunrise and sunset, I have a peanut butter sandwich. I'll also have almonds and jerky throughout the day and, always, water.

My emergence out of the canyon on the Nankoweap Trail and onto Saddle Mountain was something like Colin Fletcher's of fifty years previous, but there were no people. My hike, as intended, ended short of Point Imperial. The next day, I used the North Rim Campground shower. Clean and refreshed, and in shorts and flip-flop sandals, I drove to Point Imperial to look into the canyon where the trail is invisible to the naked eye. Two ladies approached and handed me their camera asking, "Can you snap our picture?" In my revitalized condition, no one would have ever guessed where I had just come from. I said, "Happy to ... smile." That was my rejoining of the present. From the Colorado River it was fourteen miles back to the North Rim on the Nank. When I got back on top of Saddle Mountain I could peer out into the basin between the trees of the forested rim to where the Colorado River ought to be, flowing deep down and caged up in its channel. I could now also study the canyon's topography and decipher the layout of the Nankoweap Trail. The trail is so faint that it is not visible from the North Rim, but now I know exactly where to look for it. Where it ought to be, for 130 years this October, the trail clings to its ledges on Saddle Mountain and then slides down the talus slopes that extend from Tilted Mesa.

While on the trail, deep down below, I could turn *it* on. *It* being the process of convincing myself that each footstep back to the North Rim felt like it carried me insignificantly closer to the rim of the canyon. This is a delusion, a figment of no apparent gain that can grip many. But the steps—always—add up. Steps turn into yards, yards into miles. Long ago on those annual group hikes with Andy, and then as a tired and footsore youngster, I didn't realize that hiking and backpacking employed the use of strategy. I just grew up with the Grand Canyon as an annual and grateful occurrence in my life. I can still hear Andy state his best hiking tactic to me from behind, "It's one foot in front of the other pal."

When I was safe and sound back on the North Rim at my pickup truck, with my feet dangling from the tailgate and eating my chili and crackers, I reflected on the challenge that was behind me and appreciated that Andy's hiking strategy still works.

Multitasking shelter. In Bright Angel Campground at the bottom of the canyon in August with a heavy monsoonal rain forecast, I test gear I might use in Grand Canyon's deeper backcountry. Not seen in this photo, I added two guy out points at the sides to better shed rain. Vented through the rear and peak, the V-Lite 2 tent model by Hi-Tech is not freestanding, which reduces its overall weight compared to freestanding dome tents. Weighing in at just under 2 pounds (without the manufacturer's metal pole), the tent has the ability to use a trekking pole to elevate its peak section. Double use of a gear item is employed to reduce overall backpack weight and gear handling.

THE CREATION OF THE NANKOWEAP TRAIL

Charles Doolittle Walcott (1850–1927)

Charles Doolittle Walcott, circa 1900.
(Photo courtesy of the Department of the Interior, U.S. Geological Survey.)

Between Vasey's Paradise on the north side of the river at river mile 32 and the Little Colorado River on the south side of the Colorado at river mile 61.5, within range of Nankoweap Canyon, Major John Wesley Powell describes what he would call Marble Canyon on August 8, 1869: "The limestone of this canyon is often polished, and makes beautiful marble. Sometimes the rocks are of many colors—white, gray, pink, and purple, with saffron tints."

August 9, 1869: "We pass many side canyons to-day that are dark, gloomy passages back into the heart of the rocks that form the plateau through which this canyon is cut. ... In this, great numbers of caves are hollowed out, and carvings are seen which suggest architectural forms, though on a scale so grand that architectural terms belittle them ... a distinctive feature of the canyon, we call it Marble Canyon."

Although knowing that the rock is sandstone and limestone, Powell describes the location as "marble" due to the rock wall's polished appearance from storm water rushing over the serrated canyon brim and down the sides of the walls "where showers have washed the sands over the cliffs." Powell would not only return to the vicinity in 1871–72, but again on a more dedicated note with Charles Doolittle Walcott a decade later, in 1882.

To gain access to what they were calling the "Nunkoweap Basin," John Wesley Powell and Charles Walcott, with several young Mormon laborers, hammered and chiseled out the narrow sections of the upper Supai Sandstone ledge region of an "old Indian trail." It was the autumn of 1882. Forming the Nankoweap Trail was done in a matter of weeks. Prior to the "old Indian trail," the path was a deer passageway from the North Rim to access the Nankoweap Creek and Colorado River and vice versa. The widening of the trail was necessary to accommodate the girth of a horse and, with speculation, the employ of mules to travel a right-of-way along the exposed and elevated ledge. This also provided, at best, a little confidence in the horses and mules that traveled the lofty route. As planned, Powell departed and Walcott, along with the laborers, entered the Nankoweap Basin.

> "The Grand Canyon ... nowhere else has the geologist an equal opportunity to study such a series of ancient sediments ... permitting of such certainty in the determination of stratigraphic position and succession."
> —Charles Doolittle Walcott

In 1882 ... We descended from the summit of the Kaibab Plateau on the north by a trail which we built down a side canyon in a direction toward the mouth of the Little Colorado River. The descent was made in the fall, and a small party of men was left with Mr. Walcott in this region of stupendous depths to make a study of the geology of an important region of labyrinthian gorges. Here, with his party, he was shut up for the winter, for it was known when we left him that snows on the summit of the plateau would prevent his return to the upper region before the sun should melt them the next spring.—John Wesley Powell

Almost immediately, the young laborers decided not to remain as the canyon became claustrophobic, causing in them a sort of "cabin fever." The young laborers departed the canyon before the accumulation of snow created snowdrifts that would prevent their exit.

Over the winter of 1882–83, Walcott blissfully endured the canyon and systematically explored and discerned the territorial geology. As Powell noted, Walcott had an entire book, meaning the canyon itself, open before him. Walcott's passion for paleontology and geology was obvious and confirmed. By the age of twenty-three, Walcott had accumulated natural materials and organized collections and had sold two of them to a petitioning Harvard University. Therefore, because of his tremendous interest, being alone and unencumbered at the bottom of the Grand Canyon was most likely not a distraction for the thirty-two-year-old scientist.

Walcott's primary assignment was to pick apart and examine each micro layer in what John Wesley Powell called in his summary the Tonto Group, which is comprised of Muav Limestone, Bright Angel Shale, and Tapeats Sandstone. In the later part of the 1800s, in geologic terms, the Grand Canyon system was called the Grand Canyon District and the strata near river level of the Inner Canyon was called the Algonkian [era] Rocks. These are the layers that rest directly on the nearly vertical Vishnu Schist above the Colorado River. Both the geologist and the paleontologist realized that there was something missing in this rocky relationship. It was plain to Powell who first recorded it in 1869, and later to Walcott in 1882, who realized what was missing—rock layers.

This erosion breach—missing rock layers—in the geologic layering pattern was blatantly obvious where the vertical rocks of Granite Gorge soar to meet the horizontal cap of Tapeats Sandstone, and Powell identified it on his scientific exploration expedition by boat on the Colorado River. Powell would call it the Great Unconformity.

This identification set the tone for further investigations and Powell, over a decade later, selected Walcott to carry out the geologic inquiry. Walcott stud-

Left to right. Sir Archibald Geikie (commemorated by Geikie Peak in the canyon), John Wesley Powell, and Charles Doolittle Walcott at Harpers Ferry, West Virginia, 1897. (Photo courtesy of the Department of the Interior, U.S. Geological Survey.)

ied the cause, history, structure, and composition in this noteworthy section of the Grand Canyon District. Also in his winter stay, Walcott would examine the Tonto Group's relationship with the regional Vishnu Schist (which it was already called), the near vertical rocks that make up the Inner Gorge and the Colorado River's channel downstream from the Nankoweap site. Walcott concentrated the intensity of his fieldwork on the Grand Canyon Supergroup of rocks then called the Algonkian Rocks. In doing so, Walcott discovered Grand Canyon's oldest fossil—the trilobite. The finding of the Cambrian to the Permian Period arthropod of ancient seas provided an attempt at the age of the Grand Canyon. Like yet to be discovered archaeological sites, there are inevitably more fossils yet to be discovered at Grand Canyon.

In the winter of 1889 through the spring of 1890, twenty years after John Wesley Powell's systematic expedition of Grand Canyon and seven years after Walcott, another survey was taken of the entire Colorado River system through Grand Canyon. However, this survey was for a proposed Inner Canyon railroad. Called the *Denver, Colorado Canyon and Pacific Railroad*, the line would run several hundred feet above the Colorado River following its natural water grade, with the idea of transporting coal from southern Colorado to southern California. The Colorado River expedition from Green River Station, Utah, to the mouth of the Colorado River was also known as the Brown Expedition (for Frank Mason Brown, entrepreneur) and the Stanton Survey (for Robert Brewster Stanton, chief engineer). Brown tagged along with the survey and sadly drowned in the river en route. After a retreat, Stanton immediately regrouped and out of respect for Brown and a profound belief in the project, returned to complete the survey.

In June of 1961, another explorer, archaeologist Douglas Schwartz, traversed the twenty miles of riverbank between Nankoweap Creek and Delta (river mile 52.2) and the Unkar Creek and Delta (river mile 72.5). In his report, "Nankoweap to Unkar: An Archaeological Survey of the Upper Grand Canyon," Schwartz aimed to compare "aboriginal" perseverant lifestyles at the bottom of the canyon with sites located far above and on both sides of the river. He compared such sites found along the river with such South Rim sites as Harold Gladwin's and Emil Haury's previously excavated 1936 Tusayan Ruin site. The stabilized ruin and museum site can be readily visited today on the South Rim along Arizona State Route 64, three miles west of the East Entrance Station on Grand Canyon National Park's highway section interchangeably called Desert View Drive and the East Rim Drive.

Those that travel the Nankoweap Trail today might wonder how such a (beautifully) rickety trail could support such large animals as horses and mules and the bulky equipment that Walcott packed down into the canyon. The route when it was brand new was most likely rickety in the first place as it was constructed just wide enough, with the ability to support an equipment load, in a matter of weeks to provide quick access to the region. What would become of the passage after Walcott was finished was likely inconsequential, as his job would be complete. Today, the "old Indian trail" improvement is over 130 years old, and the unmaintained right-of-way has eroded and fallen into the depths of the canyon. It is now up to the hiker to keep the trail traceable with cairns that are stacked high enough to be seen from below on the ascent of the trail—through brush and over ridges.

Walcott joined the United States Geological Survey in 1879 and would succeed John Wesley Powell as its director in 1894, and at the same time the Nankoweap Trail would acquire a new flavor, a character of the Old West, as the northern passage of the Horsethief Trail.

Robert Brewster Stanton, 1907.
Stanton found himself emotionally and visually captivated by Grand Canyon: "As we climbed the hillsides, we found wild flowers in full bloom, with new spring grass three inches high, and birds of many kinds singing on almost every bush. In the early morning the spray from the [river] waves had frozen in a sheet of ice over our coats ... the wind was blowing in great gusts and whirling the dry sand from shore into our eyes. The wind storm ceased, but at night it began to rain, and we slept till near morning in a steady pour, with only our bed canvas drawn up over our heads." Though the oar-powered boat journey of the river was challenging, arduous, and life defeating for a few, enamored Robert Stanton also greatly enjoyed traveling Grand Canyon's nomadic ways.

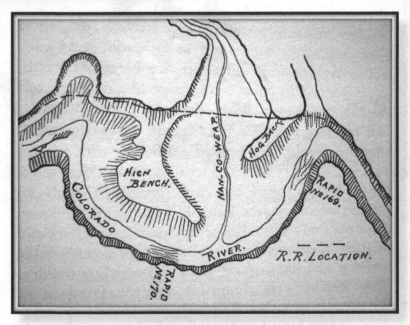

Railroad location at Nankoweap. Robert Stanton's topological map of the mouth of Nankoweap Canyon and Creek, January 18, 1890. Notations: the "HIGH BENCH" is Nankoweap Mesa and the "HOGBACK" palisade is Barbenceta Butte. The dotted line is the proposed right-of-way. The river is flowing sketch left. If the railroad was constructed, the tracts would have passed over Nankoweap Mesa and Barbenceta Butte and between the two, Stanton would schedule his engineering passion—a single span bridge.

The Horsethief Trail: A Notorious Trans-Canyon Trail System

After Charles Walcott left the canyon, the route may have fallen into disuse for only a short time. Once word drifted out that there was a "new" trail on the north side of the canyon built by explorer and geologist John Wesley Powell, the route found itself useful again by prospectors and their Prohibition-era stills. In 1928, Grand Canyon National Park's first naturalist, Glen Sturdevant, discovered en route on the Tanner Trail an abandoned distillation encampment complete with a medley of bottles, several kegs, and rusting tools.

"Away From Saddle Mountain." Desperados spiriting livestock through House Rock Valley. Ink on white paper by the author.

There was no time to lose. The bandits were being followed. Knowing that they were under pursuit, rustlers would position themselves along the route below the rims in the rock outcroppings to encounter a posse at more than one strategic ambush location, called a *robber's roost.*

Before the bootleggers, rumrunners, and moonshiners, it didn't take long for horse thieves to put two and two together and realize what innovative venture they might have on the North Rim's Nankoweap Trail and the South Rim's Tanner Trail (then known as the Tanner-French Trail for Seth Tanner and Franklin French). Notoriously, the two trails and a river crossing took on a new itinerary. Rustling was a lot of work even for rustlers. Horses were spirited down the Tanner and up the Nankoweap and vice versa. However, the key to using the Grand Canyon to obscure the rustling activity and transport stock was in the ability to water the animals. Once away from the Colorado River, in a terrain where water is scarce, the stock had to get to the next known watering hole.

Rustlers could get away with the severe meagerness of en route graze and fatten the horses up once on either rim prior to "market," but the horses needed water to survive the hot and rugged canyon. At the Colorado River at the end of the Tanner Trail, the long summer days in the wide open canyon and the hot Inner Gorge never give the beach area a chance to cool down. Summer temperatures are 130 degrees where the rock and sand accumulate the heat of the Inner Canyon day. The following day it starts all over again. The result of the daily summer cycle has earned the sand dunes at Tanner Beach the popular nickname Furnace Flats. I'm sure that rustlers had a word back in their day for Tanner Beach that was something less glamorous.

On the south side of the river from the end of the Tanner Trail, livestock was driven along today's Beamer Trail, which travels east to west within access of the Colorado River. But once across the river, moving the herd required the skill of the rustler to provide water. It is thought that rustlers were one-time miners who surrendered mining to the canyon and took on rustling. Prospecting pits and kitchen utensils reveal that miners were working the Nankoweap Basin, testing the earth for mineral wealth. Hearty enough and weathered to bare the burdens of an Inner Canyon lifestyle, it was the miner who knew better than anyone else where the canyon's hidden permanent creeks and springs and seeps could be found.

According to Grand Canyon's legendary backcountry hiker, Harvey Butchart, most Colorado River crossings took place near the McCormick Mine and the Little Colorado River. At Palisades Creek on the south side of the river, where the river ran a bit shallow and a bit narrow, the horses were forded to Lava Canyon and Creek on the north bank. Even in the spring when the river wasn't flowing shallow, the livestock were obligated to cross the river's dangerous currents. There was no time to lose. The bandits were being followed. Knowing that they were under pursuit, rustlers would position themselves along the route below the rims in the rock outcroppings to encounter a posse at more than one strategic ambush location, called a *robber's roost*. A storming posse knew it could not

River crossing. The Little Colorado River entering the Colorado River mainstream from the southeast. Photo taken from Cape Solitude, South Rim. (GRCA D1730)

Robber's roost. On the other side of a sheer cliff face or from above on a ledge, bandits laid in wait for a posse. The self portrait of the author near Marion Point at the trail's Scary Spot illustrates the elusiveness of the route.

match the horse thieves' line of defense, especially on the Nankoweap Trail with its abundance of brush, trees, boulders, and cliffs that concealed the bandits' whereabouts and their diverse arsenal ranging from bullets to a pickoff armed with cobblestones.

Once across the river, the route ran with variations in a northeasterly direction following the perennial creek water of Lava and Kwagunt Canyons. Accomplished in sections, the route on the north side of the river ran from Lava Canyon to Carbon Canyon to Sixty-Mile Canyon to and through the valley of Awatubi Crest to Malgosa Canyon to Kwagunt Canyon and, at last, arriving at Nankoweap Creek. But the rigorous journey was not over. In some respects it had just begun. From Nankoweap Creek at the bottom of the Nankoweap Trail, the waterless journey continued to the North Rim—where there was still

> "The use of firearms with swiftness and accuracy was necessary in the calling of the desperado, after fate had marked him and set him apart for the inevitable, though possibly long-deferred, end."
> —Emerson Hough, 1907

no water. The bandits had to make it into the meadows of the North Rim where they could utilize the standing water in the limestone sinks, such as those at Van Slack & Thompson and Indian Lakes, located south of Jacob Lake, adjacent to present-day Arizona State Route 67—the approach to Grand Canyon National Park's North Rim Entrance Station. Eventually, rustlers discovered some of the concealed water sources on the North Rim, such as Robbers Roost Spring, adjacent to today's highway 67 in The Basin of Outlet Canyon.

Hollowed-out. Watering trough on the North Rim at Robber's Roost Spring, 1961. (GRCA 4117B)

Deer Lake. In DeMotte Park on the North Rim, one of the few possible "watering holes" for rustled horses.

Between the acquisition and the sale of rustled livestock, brands had to be promptly changed. Altering brands was most likely carried out in the confines of the canyon once a pursuing posse was no longer at bay. Altering brands was considered an art by fellow rustlers. The original brand would be changed into an entirely new trademark. Lines, numbers, symbols, and curves would be added with a stoking red-hot "runnin' iron." The running iron was a branding tool forged into the form of a straight poker, or the same rod with a hook or loop at one end. Superior to the running iron was a glowing red-hot saddle cinch ring or a simple piece of telegraph wire that would only lightly scar and blend with the old brand. Telegraph wire could be bent into almost any shape to modify a registered brand.

Horses that were previously stolen were routinely plundered back from the new owners and trafficked back across the canyon, where the brands were altered yet again, and then again resold. The horses selected for theft, if possible, had simple brands that could easily be re-branded and then re-branded again with few design complications. It was a rancher's vicious cycle. Big outfits, such as the Babbitt Brothers, stood a better chance of recognizing their stock with altered brands over smaller outfits.

Arizona did not receive its statehood status until February 14, 1912. In the Grand Canyon region, rustlers stole horses in the Arizona Territory with the intent of selling the stock in Utah. Because Utah was already a state, or transitioning to its January 4, 1896 statehood, it may have been more manageable for rustlers to confuse matters more by mix-matching brands in either state or territory.

Some rustlers evolved from the cowboy who was employed to round up strays—mavericks—livestock that was considered expendable should they become detached from the herd or lost. Cowboys saw this type of rustling as a way to get an easy start in the horse and cattle ranching business. By simply rounding up any and all strays, they could build up a herd and a brand of their own.

Outside or within the law, those that traveled immediately after Walcott kept the Nankoweap Trail's pathway clear enough for others to follow—no different than the intermittent hikers of today who follow the upper ledge-ways and the lower talus slopes to Nankoweap Creek and the Colorado River.

Hikers discover for themselves evidence of a Native American past. By way of potsherds and projectile points, rock art and split-twig figurines, cliff storage granaries and dwellings, and bridges constructed of pre-historic driftwood that was placed over crevasses to efficiently create shortcuts to the upper terraces and mesas above the Colorado River—a way of life that was once for the Ancestral Puebloan.

Bypassing a crevasse. The stick and stone bridge-way, called Anasazi Bridge, created an ancient short cut in Marble Canyon making an efficient route to the North Rim. Location undisclosed to preserve site integrity. (GRCA)

The Kiva in the Sand

Just what may be under the Colorado River's beach sand at the Nankoweap Delta may be indicative of the archaeological findings 13 river miles downstream near the historic Horsethief Trail crossing on the south side of the river at Palisades Creek. First documented in 1978 and tribally called *Anasazi*, an archaeological site near the transition zone of Marble Canyon and the Colorado River's Inner Gorge was discovered by the crew of a National Park Service patrol boat.

Glimpses of cobblestone masonry protruding up through the sand proved that a site was looming down below. However, limited funding

> With the boats moored and the archaeological team fully equipped, a two-session reconnaissance of the site, which was waiting centuries for discovery, awaited no longer.

prohibited an excavation of the site and it remained undisturbed, in preservation by the grains of sand and time. It would be thirty more years until the site could be credibly excavated.

In 1995, seventeen years later, with better funding and recognizing the importance of this archeological event in the bottom of the canyon, modest check dams and small but significant stabilization efforts of the site were carried out. This task was not only essential, but urgent. The hewing arroyo made by Palisades Creek was harrowing and growing to a point that threatened the site.

Four years passed and in 1999, minor exploratory excavations took place at the feature most affected by the creek's gullying processes. At the time, archaeologists revealed the topical curving crest of a masonry wall. Once again, lack of funding limited excavation and the site could only be intermittently attended to. The excavation was abandoned, but a team would return. To catch up with its modern definition, the setting was re-termed an "Ancestral Puebloan" site.

An·a·sá·zi is Navajo (Diné) variably meaning "ancient enemy" or "enemy ancestor" and was assigned by Richard Wetherill, rancher turned archaeologist from Mancos, Colorado, to refer to the people of the Southwest's mesas and canyons. The term is erroneous to the Hopi, who claim direct ancestry and who prefer the term Hisatsinom, meaning "old ones" or "ancestors." Anasazi is still in use today as a scholarly term and by the public, but it is in transition to several expressions including Ancestral Puebloan and Prehistoric Puebloan.

In May 2008, nine years after the 1999 team's departure, archaeologists with the Museum of Northern Arizona and the National Park Service floated the Colorado River to the riparian archaeological site. With the boats moored and the archaeological team fully equipped, a two-session reconnaissance of the site was started. The archaeologists could now finally determine the extent of the exposed cobblestones.

As the explorers carefully removed the earth and the sand dune vault over the twenty days that they were there, rooms and storage chambers and hearths built of masonry, and artifacts reposing under the sand dunes of the river's bank, were discovered. The momentous event revealed a continuous curved wall, and it was now obvious to the searchers that they were uncovering a kiva—a subterranean ceremonial room found within Ancestral Puebloan archaeological sites and in settings such as the ancient and continuously occupied Hopi settlement of Oraibi, located to the east of Grand Canyon.

The meaning of a site that includes a kiva is significant. Kivas have a small-diameter depression or hole in the floor that is sometimes lined with pottery shards. This is the *Sipapu*—the gateway to and from the spirit world. The presence of a kiva speaks of a long-term existence of generations of a people or the coming-and-going of individual tribes who used the earthen chamber to address and confer on the traditional epic stories and heroic legends that distinguish their way of life.

The kiva was essential. To keep crops growing long after the storms had passed, dances were performed inside the kiva to keep rain falling below the dark thunderhead clouds. After dark and far into the night, dancing kachinas performed inside the kiva, which had a small fire burning near its center. Kachinas are portrayed by certain members of the Hopi tribe, who are qualified to wear appropriate masks and dress that represent such spirits as animals. While firelight highlighted the feathered costumes and the dancers' painted bodies, shadows played against the walls of the kiva and between the rungs of the wood beam ladder descending from the roof. Dances still occur from the end of December to mid-July. The Hopi believe that during the summer and winter solstices, the

Kiva in the sand. Palisades Creek kiva. Photo by Tom Bartel. (GRCA)

kachinas pass on to their own spirit world by way of *Huehanapatcha*, the "The Snow Covered Mountains"—today's San Francisco Peaks of Flagstaff, Arizona.

Back at the site, the variety of black-on-white and other variegated pottery shards, along with projectile points discovered in the sand, will help archaeologists identify whether the people who lived along the river's bank had migrating relations with other peoples to the east and west. Compared to the bustling occupation of the area almost a thousand years ago, today the remote Palisades Creek region is seldom visited except by the occasional river party who may stop at the creek and the few backpackers who travel—and endure—the Inner Canyon's southern section of the Horsethief Trail (collectively the Tanner and Beamer Trails) in the vicinity of the Little Colorado River. These are located below the rugged South Rim region of Desert View, 25 miles east of Grand Canyon Village.

Folsom projectile point. Artifact found in the Nankoweap area in 1993. The first "Folsom" point was discovered near Folsom, New Mexico, in 1927, in the bone structure of a bison. (GRCA 14051)

Except to the trained eye, the rare visitor to this remote area of Grand Canyon National Park will not find a trace of the Ancestral Puebloan dwelling site and its twelve-foot diameter Palisades Creek kiva. In accordance with the National Park Service's mandate to preserve the Grand Canyon's wilderness, and in partnership with the Vanishing Treasures Program to protect archaeological sites, the ruin was once again buried under the sand dunes for its best chance of preservation. Below the South Rim's Comanche Point, where the surface of the ground was re-contoured and re-vegetated, it appears as if the archaeologists, their tools, and their enthusiasm were never there.

Careful placement. Small and just a few inches square, split-twig figurines resemble deer or maybe desert bighorn sheep and are typically discovered under rock cairns high up in the canyon walls in nearly inaccessible and unoccupied remote caves. This one was discovered in Marble Canyon near the Nankoweap region. Sometimes the figurines are penetrated through their side with a pointed stick—or spear—possibly for the hopes of a successful hunt. A figurine without the spear is plausibly the hope of the Ancestral Puebloan for a herd that would sustain the tribe. Alternatively, the figurine effigy could represent the animal's final burial or resting place after a hunt. (GRCA 4684)

USGS FORMATION REGISTRY: NANKOWEAP BASIN

Alsap Butte: Elevation 7,494 feet; 7 aerial miles northeast of Grand Canyon Lodge. John T. Alsap (1832–1886) was Arizona's first territorial treasurer, judge, lawyer, and town commissioner. Through his influence, Maricopa County was created.

Bourke Point: Elevation 6,542 feet; 7.5 aerial miles northeast of Grand Canyon Lodge. John Gregory Bourke (1846–1896) was an Arizona historian and cavalry captain who attended campaigns against the Bedonkohe Apache Geronimo (Goyaalé: "one who yawns" [1829–1909]) under the command of General George Crook. During such episodes, Bourke methodically recorded the customs of the Indians he observed. Crook recognized Bourke's aptitude and from 1880–1881 commissioned him to study and document the Navajo (Diné) and Apache lifestyles.

Butchart Butte: (newer designation; not on USGS maps). Elevation 7,601 feet; 7 aerial miles northeast of Grand Canyon Lodge. The butte is named for legendary Grand Canyon hiker John Harvey Butchart (1907–2002). Harvey Butchart holds the record for the most first ascents of the Inner Canyon's butte, temple, and sky island formations. Butchart also logged more than 12,000 Inner Canyon miles in his relationship with Grand Canyon, which began in 1945 on the South Kaibab Trail. His hiking logs where made into books, encouraged by La Siesta Press's Walt Wheelock, in 1976 and were available through the National Park Service's Grand Canyon National Park South Rim Visitor Center. The trail books were the first of their kind that, as Harvey would say, "sportingly" described remote Inner Canyon trails, routes, and passages. Hikers who utilized Harvey's terse Grand Canyon trail guides in the late 1970s and early '80s paid attention when he stated that a passage was "sporting"—Harvey's way of saying *Beware*.

Colter Butte: Elevation 7,256 feet; 7 aerial miles northeast of Grand Canyon Lodge. The butte is named for James G.H. Colter (1844–1922). He was a lumberman by trade by the age of twenty, with three two-horse teams that he brought from Wisconsin and a mower and reaper that he purchased in Atchison, Kansas. Colter arrived in 1872 at the Little Colorado River, Arizona Territory, and the region of today's Springerville, Arizona, where he grew barley to support the operations of the U.S. Cavalry stationed at Fort Apache.

Ehrenberg Point: Elevation 6,960 feet; 6.5 aerial miles northeast of Grand Canyon Lodge. The point is named for emigrant Herman Christian Ehrenberg (circa 1810–1866). Born in Germany, Ehrenberg was a mining engineer and surveyor. With Charles Poston (Poston is commemorated in the Grand Canyon with Poston Butte), Ehrenberg plotted the town of Colorado City (present-day Yuma, Arizona). In commemoration, residents of Mineral City (formerly Olive City) at Bradshaw's Ferry (where passengers and supplies from San Bernardino, California, were transported to La Paz, Arizona) renamed their town Ehrenberg. As an official of the Sonora Exploring and Mining Company, Ehrenberg co-authored an article in the newspaper *Arizonan* attacking culprits of violence in west Arizona Territory in 1861. Almost prophetically, Ehrenberg wrote: "Every mine is baptized in blood. What country and business can prosper under such monstrous activity? And what man would settle his family in these blood drenched valleys?" On October 9, 1866, Ehrenberg died under ambush by a Chimehuevi Indian near Auga Caliente, California (present-day Palm Springs). Michael Goldwater and his son Baron (father of Barry Goldwater) discovered and buried Ehrenberg's body at the Dos Palmas (Rancho) Stagecoach Station. Many believe that Ehrenberg was killed by a "renegade Indian," while others maintain that the proprietor of the station, W.H. Smith, took Ehrenberg's life as Ehrenberg was possibly in possession of roughly $4,000 in gold.

Hancock Butte: Elevation 6,780 feet; 6.5 aerial miles northeast of Grand Canyon Lodge. The butte is named for Captain William Augustus Hancock (1831–1902) who was hired to survey and grid the town site of the Salt River Valley's Phoenix, where in 1870 he also built the first structure.

Kwagunt Butte: Elevation 6,377 feet; 12 aerial miles northeast of Grand Canyon Lodge. Major John Wesley Powell named the butte and surrounding area formations for Southern Paiute Kwagunt (also spelled Kivagunt). In 1869, Kwagunt told Powell that he owned all the land in the area because his father had given it to him.

Kwagunt Creek: Elevation 2,800 feet at the Colorado River and confluence.

Marion Point: Elevation 5,600 feet; 9.5 aerial miles northeast of Grand Canyon Lodge, North Rim. Named for John Marion (1835–1891), an Arizona pioneer, legislator, and editor of the Prescott *Arizona Miner* and the Prescott *Courier*.

Mt. Hayden: Elevation 8,372 feet; 7 aerial miles northeast of Grand Canyon Lodge. The spire formation is named for Charles Trumbull Hayden (1825–1900) who founded a flour mill and river ferry service across the Salt River (near the city of Phoenix which was incorporated in 1881) in an area that became known as Hayden's Ferry (today's Tempe, Arizona).

Nankoweap Butte: Elevation 5,430 feet; 10.5 aerial miles northeast of Grand Canyon Lodge. The formation is drained by Nankoweap and Kwagunt Creeks.

Nankoweap Creek: Elevation at the Colorado River 2,802 feet, 7.5 aerial miles northeast of Grand Canyon Lodge. The Nankoweap Trail creek section is 3 miles long from the trail's junction to the Colorado River. The creek bed is of silty basalt, which may make searching for the upstream spring source a flavorsome option. As of October 2012, the creek directly at the ascent junction was flowing vigorous and clear.

Nankoweap Mesa: Elevation gradient 6,063 feet northerly, 6,000 feet mid-mesa, 6,242 feet southerly; 12 aerial miles northeast of Grand Canyon Lodge. The formation is 1.5 miles long by .4 mile wide and is drained by Nankoweap Creek

> **Nankoweap**
> Many North Rim region place names end with the syllable "weap." The term is from the North Rim's Southern Paiute, with "weap" (pronounced "weep") referring to a locale with several meanings, such as valley, wash, gorge, or canyon. Nankoweap in its entirety means "canyon of echoes" and variously "humans killed," making reference to an ancient battle in the North Rim area between Indian parties at the "head of Nancoweap" [sic].

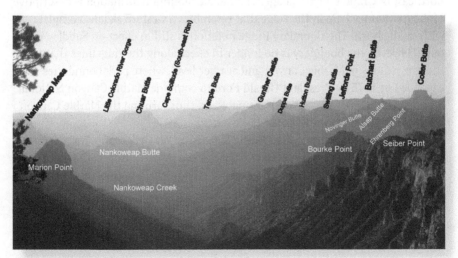

Formation identification. From the Inner Canyon on the Nankoweap Trail near Marion Point.

to the north and Kwagunt Creek to the south. The site houses the Nankoweap Ruin on the lower northeast cliffs.

Nankoweap Rapids: Elevation 2,802 feet at the Colorado River and Nankoweap Delta; 7.5 aerial miles from Grand Canyon Lodge. The rapid is rated as 3–4 or "medium" and is one of the longest rapids in the canyon. At river level, the view up into Nankoweap Canyon provides a view of the North Rim at Point Imperial.

Novinger Butte: Elevation 6,880 feet; 7.5 aerial miles northeast of Grand Canyon Lodge. Arizona territorial pioneer Simon Novinger (1832–1904) arrived at the Salt River Valley in 1871 by the time Phoenix had its first two buildings. Novinger was a prospector with two partners. Late one afternoon, while the partners were out searching for water, Novinger was attacked by six Indians "whom he put to flight." In the attack, he was wounded in the right leg and ultimately made his recovery at Fort McDowell. He returned to the Phoenix area in 1873, where he staked and filed a mining claim. By 1877, in the growth path of Phoenix and departing the aspects of mining, the Novinger Ranch grew hay and grain.

Point Imperial: Elevation 8,803 feet; 7 aerial miles northeast of Grand Canyon Lodge. Point Imperial was formerly named Skidoo Point, as it was a tourist's typical last view of the canyon, as in "all there is to do now is skidoo." In 1911, with Allan Doyle, historian Sharlot Hall described the Inner Canyon from Point Imperial as what the moonscape must be like.

Saddle Mountain and Boundary Ridge: Elevation 8,424 feet; 9.5 aerial miles northeast of Grand Canyon Lodge. The Saddle Mountain formation is descriptive of the pronounced dip in the ridge that resembles a western saddle, complete with saddle horn. The Boundary Ridge notation is still in effect on Saddle Mountain. However, the boundary is no longer in effect along the ridgelines that form the rim regions of Marble Canyon and at river level, where park boundaries were expanded in 1975 by President Gerald Ford to combine Marble Canyon National Monument with Grand Canyon National Park, thus forming the Marble Canyon section of Grand Canyon National Park.

Seiber Point [sic]: [as spelled by the U.S. Board on Geographic Naming and on U.S.G.S. maps]. Elevation 6,800 feet; 9.5 aerial miles northeast of Grand Canyon Lodge, North Rim. Named for Al Sieber (1844–1907), an Indian scout under the command of General George Crook.

Sullivan Peak: Elevation 8,320 feet; 6.5 aerial miles northeast of Grand Canyon Lodge. The formation is named for Arizona territorial pioneer Jerry Sullivan (1843–1929), a cattleman who founded the O-O brand working up a mass herd of cattle and horses. Understanding civic relationships through the ranching business, Sullivan became a state legislator in Yavapai County. For a time he was also a director of the Bank of Arizona.

Tilted Mesa: Elevation (gradient) 6,799 feet east to 5,999 feet west (1 aerial mile long by .5 mile wide); 11 aerial miles northeast of Grand Canyon Lodge. Named in 1927 by cartographer François Matthes for its oblique peninsula that attaches to Saddle Mountain.

Woolsey Butte: Elevation 7,200 feet; 7.5 aerial miles northeast of Grand Canyon Lodge. Named for Arizona pioneer King Samuel Woolsey (1832–1879), who was a teamster and road builder and established the Agua Fria Ranch near present-day Dewey-Humboldt, Arizona, on Big Bug Creek. Woolsey was accused of brutal attacks as an Indian fighter. However, he was subject to attacks by Indians at his ranch. Woolsey's initial encounter with Tonto Apaches was with two ranch hands that had returned with a buckboard full of hay. Becoming outnumbered and surrounded, Woolsey stood motionless, and probably breathless, facing the tribe with a double-barrel shotgun, reputedly his only weapon. Woolsey deferred any action until the moment the chief came within a few paces—and fired. The chief was killed instantly and the tribe disbanded. Woolsey's ranch became a central base from which militia would head south and east into the Superstition Mountains in a conflict that would last almost two decades.

Sidekicks. Because of sparse vegetation, cattle herds in the House Rock Valley are kept relatively small.

REGIONAL CONTACTS

Enter key words for websites

Backcountry Information Center: Grand Canyon National Park, South Rim, P.O. Box 129, Grand Canyon, AZ 86023; (928) 638-7875 (line answered 1 p.m.–5 p.m. Monday-Friday); Grand Canyon National Park **general information:** (928) 638-7888; **website: nps.gov/grca**; Backcountry Office, North Rim, located in Grand Canyon National Park on Hwy 67 north of visitor services.

DeMotte Park Campground: Highway 67 (6 miles north of the North Rim Entrance Station at Mile Post 605); 38 sites; drinking water; toilet. Accommodates tents, trailers, motor homes (no utility hookups or dump station). Contact: North Kaibab Ranger District or Kaibab Plateau Visitor Center.

Grand Canyon Lodge (historic North Rim lodge): Hwy 67 in Grand Canyon National Park, North Rim, at Bright Angel Point. Reservations: (877) 386-4383. Contact summer (May–October): (928) 638-2611; contact winter (November–April): (928) 645-6865.

Backcountry Office, North Rim. Located north of visitor services, arrive at least a day in advance of a hike into the canyon, or when exploring the rims, to seek precise weather and route conditions.

North Rim icon. Grand Canyon Lodge, located on the brink of the canyon adjacent-west of Bright Angel Point at the terminus of the National Park Service administered section of Arizona State Route 67.

Jacob Lake Inn: Hwy 89A & AZ-67, Jacob Lake, AZ 86022; (928) 643-7232.

Kaibab Lodge: Highway 67 (6 miles north of the North Rim Entrance Station at Mile Post 605); Seasonal operation based on northern Arizona weather patterns; (928) 638-2389.

Kaibab Plateau Visitor Center (North Rim): P.O. Box 17, Fredonia, AZ 86022; (928) 643-7298.

North Kaibab Ranger District (North Rim): P.O. Box 248, Fredonia, AZ 86022; (928) 643-7395.

North Rim Campground: inside Grand Canyon National Park. 75 sites that allow up to six people, two vehicles, and three tents; 12 tent-only sites, 3 group sites. Reservations are made through National Recreation Reservation Services, (877) 444-6777.

North Rim Country Store: Highway 67 (6 miles north of the North Rim Entrance Station at Mile Post 605); seasonal dates based on northern Arizona weather patterns. Fuel: unleaded and diesel; grocery, water, maps, camper needs, propane filling, tire repair; (928) 638-9358.

In Utah within close proximity of Jacob Lake and the North Rim

Comfort Inn: 815 East Highway 89, Kanab, UT 84741; (435) 644-8888.

True Value Hardware: 227 East 300 South (located on Hwy 89), Kanab, UT 84741; (435) 644-2779.

Willow Creek Outdoor (outfitter, hiking gear): 263 South 100 East (located on Hwy 89) Kanab, UT 84741; (435) 644-8884.

High country outpost. Located at the junction of U.S. 89A and Highway 67 at the elevation of 7925 feet, Jacob Lake Inn is the final year-round supply and fuel destination before departure to North Rim explorations.

Jacob Lake Inn neighbor. The Kaibab Plateau Visitor Center houses an area-knowledgeable staff, books, and maps.

Up-to-date forest and road information. The station is located in Fredonia, Arizona, on U.S 89A south of Arizona State Route 389.

Old-timer. No longer in service and located westerly of the Jacob Lake Inn, the Jacob Lake Ranger Station was built in 1910 as a base for visitor contact and horseback ranger patrol in the Kaibab Forest, North Rim.